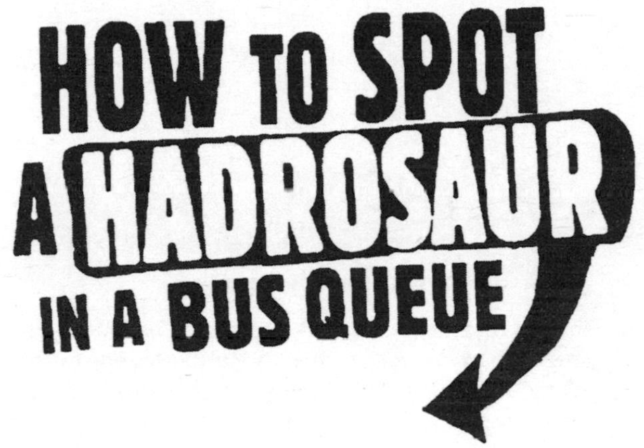
HOW TO SPOT
A HADROSAUR
IN A BUS QUEUE

ANDY SEED

h
A division of Hodder Headline Limited

Acknowledgements

Large thanks to my fine wife, Barbara, for her ideas and for listening to my twaddle, and to Rob Falconer for his 'interesting' input. I'm also highly indebted to Anne Clark, Paula Borton and Katie Sergeant at Hodder for their wise guidance and kind patience.

About the author

Andy Seed used to teach in a primary school but now writes funny poetry and dull books for teachers, as well as collecting useless facts. At other times he designs games and enters caption competitions (of which he has won over 100). Andy's past achievements include playing football for The Rest of The World (a college five-a-side team), and his ambition is to learn how to yodel. He is tall, ungainly and married with three kids. *How to Spot a Hadrosaur in a Bus Queue* is Andy's first book for children.

Editor: Katie Sergeant
Book design by Andy Summers
Cover design: Hodder Children's Books

Published in Great Britain in 2004
by Hodder Children's Books

A catalogue record for this book is available from the British Library.

10 9 8 7 6 5 4 3 2 1

ISBN: 0340893036

Printed and bound by Bookmarque Ltd, Croydon, Surrey

The paper and board used in this paperback by Hodder Children's Books are natural recyclable products made from wood grown in sustainable forests. The manufacturing processes conform to the environmental regulations of the country of origin.

Hodder Children's Books
A division of Hodder Headline Limited
338 Euston Road, London NW1 3BH

To Joe, Ben and Naomi

Fake snot recipe

1 Add 2 tablespoons of borax powder to 1/2 litre of warm water in a bottle with a lid
2 Shake well and allow to cool
3 Add 2 spoonfuls of water to 3 spoonfuls of PVA glue in a bowl
4 Stir well
5 Add 2-3 drops of green food colouring
6 Stir, then add the borax mixture
7 Stir again and you have lots of snot

Charles Dickens' characters

Character	Book
Honeythunder	*The Mystery of Edwin Drood*
Sweedlepipe	*Martin Chuzzlewit*
Muddlebranes	*Sketches by Boz*
Mr Podsnap	*Our Mutual Friend*
Noddy Boffin	*Our Mutual Friend*
Fezziwig	*A Christmas Carol*
M'Choakumchild	*Hard Times*
Kit Nubbles	*The Old Curiosity Shop*
Mr Slurk	*Pickwick Papers*
Sophie Wackles	*The Old Curiosity Shop*

15 things that don't exist

1. Treacle mines
2. Atlantis
3. Unicorns
4. A £7 note
5. The equator
6. Spaghetti trees
7. Vampires
8. Smellovision
9. Middle Earth
10. Ned Flanders
11. Left-handed screwdrivers
12. Dragons
13. Light sabres
14. 30th February
15. Tartan paint

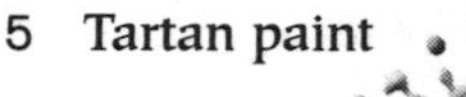

Max ball speeds

Pelota	303 km/h (188 mph)
Golf	274 km/h (170 mph)
Badminton	261 km/h (162 mph)
Squash	243 km/h (151 mph)
Tennis	240 km/h (149 mph)
Hockey	193 km/h (120 mph)
Table tennis	171 km/h (106 mph)
Baseball	166 km/h (103 mph)
Cricket	261 km/h (100 mph)
Football	140 km/h (87 mph)

When to see shooting stars

Meteor shower	Date	Max meteors per hour
Quadrantids	3-4 Jan	100
Lyrids	22 Apr	10
Delta Aquarids	31 Jul	25
Perseids	12 Aug	100
Orionids	21 Oct	20
Taurids	8 Nov	10
Leonids	17 Nov	10
Geminids	14 Dec	50
Ursids	22 Dec	15

Cranky pub names

Howl at the Moon	(Liverpool)
The Barking Shark	(Haverfordwest)
My Father's Moustache	(Aberdeen)
The Moose Hoose	(Kilmarnock)
The Bleeding Wolf	(Stoke)
Ye Olde Trip to Jerusalem	(Nottingham)
The Barmy Arms	(London)
Oily Johnnies Inn	(Winscales)
The One-Eyed Rat	(Ripon)
The Coal Hole	(London)
The Lazy Toad	(Shoreham-by-Sea)
Ye Olde Cheshire Cheese	(London)
The Smack Inn	(Whitstable)
The World's End	(Tilbury)
Q	(Stalybridge)

Disgusting world cuisine

UK	Tripe (cow's stomach lining)
Indonesia	Smoked bats
Italy	Roast thrush
China	Rat stew
SE Asia	Fish eyes
USA	Chicken feet soup
Africa	Fresh blood
Mediterranean	Sheep's head
Sardinia	Maggot cheese
India	Cow urine
Hong Kong	Monkey brains

Ghosties

- Ghoul
- Spectre
- Spook
- Apparition
- Shade
- Phantom
- Shadow
- Wraith
- Spirit
- Vision

SILLY FACTS

Who would win the fight?

Ant	v.	slug	Ant
Jellyfish	v.	vampire bat	Bat
Siberian tiger	v.	Florence Nightingale	Tiger
Killer whale	v.	Transit van	Van
Pensioner	v.	garlic sausage	Pensioner
Pie	v.	chips	Pie
Coat hanger	v.	box of tissues	Coat hanger
A tornado	v.	Bolton	Draw

BIG dams

Name	Place	Height
Hoover	USA	221 m
Chivor	Colombia	237 m
Mica	Canada	244 m
Vajont	Italy	262 m
Inguri	Georgia	272 m
Rogun	Russia	335 m

Mountain biking glossary

Bacon	Scabs on a rider's elbows and knees
Boing-boing	Bike with front and rear suspension
Cloon	Slamming into the ground
Death cookies	Large rocks which cause the bike to jerk about
Face plant	Hitting the ground face first; also called an 'auger' or 'soil sample'
Granny gear	A bike's lowest gear, used for difficult uphill sections
Grunt	A steep climb requiring the use of the granny gear
Involuntary dismount	A crash
Over-the-bar blood donor	A rider injured after a big endo (jamming on the front brake so that the back of the bike flies up)

Eight racehorses of 2002

- Zoom Zoom
- Quite a Case
- Snip Snap
- My Giddy Aunt
- King of Peru
- Biff-em
- Hufflepuf
- Big Bad Bob

'rhoid buffing	When a rider's botty hits the rear wheel on a steep downhill blast
Superman	A rider who doesn't land for ages after flying over the handlebars
Taco	A severe wheel bend caused by an accident
Trail swag	Equipment dropped by other riders
Unobtanium	A non-existent metal used to describe an ultra hi-tech bike
Vegetable tunnel	A heavily overgrown track which requires the rider to duck a lot
Wild pigs	Squealy brakes

11 skipping rhymes

- 'Teddy bear, teddy bear'
- 'Little bumper car'
- 'I like coffee, I like tea'
- 'Apples, peaches, pears and plums'
- 'Miss Mary Mack'
- 'Would you marry me?'
- 'Down by the river'
- 'Ice cream soda'
- 'Salt, mustard, vinegar, pepper'
- 'Baby's in the cradle'
- 'Keep the kettle boiling'

Strange hats

1 The best top hats are made of beaver fur
2 A chef's hat should have 100 pleats
3 In 1732 the Hat Act made it illegal to bring American hats into Britain
4 Panama hats are only made in Ecuador
5 Abraham Lincoln's hat size was $7\frac{1}{8}$
6 A ten-gallon hat actually holds 0.75 gallons
7 Two-tone suede skull caps cost $4 each

Things you can buy with £1 million

150,000 kg of houmous

$6\frac{1}{2}$ Ferrari 575s

2 Spanish castles

0.02 of Zinedine Zidane

20,000 pairs of Doc Martens

50 grand pianos

33,300 km (20,693 miles) of fishing line

4 small helicopters

2,500 ostriches

80,000 *Bob the Builder* DVDs

62 million pipe cleaners

140 one-kilogram gold bars

Who has the most goats
(And who hasn't)

China	149 million
India	123 million
Brazil	13 million
Bulgaria	1 million
Fiji Islands	235,000
Israel	73,000
Ireland	9,000
Liechtenstein	280

Royal nicknames

King Ethelred (England)	The Unready
Thorfin I (Norway)	The Skull Splitter
Henry VIII (England)	Bluff King Hal
Ivan IV (Russia)	The Terrible
George I (Britain)	Turnip Head
George III (Britain)	Farmer George
George IV (Britain)	Prince Charming
William IV (Britain)	Silly Billy
George VI (Britain)	Our Bertie

Burning energy

Activity	Kcal per hour (adult)
Sleeping	80
Watching TV	100
Queuing for chips	110
Typing	140
Walking to school/work	240
Riding a bike	350
Playing tennis	380
Swimming	450
Playing footie	500
Climbing stairs	600
Playing basketball	680
Jogging	780

Nine clichés beginning with 'P'

1 Pack it in
2 Pain in the neck
3 Penny for your thoughts
4 Piece of cake
5 Pie in the sky
6 Playing with fire
7 Pretty as a picture
8 Pull yourself together
9 Put your money where your mouth is

Shepherd's score for counting sheep

1 Yan
2 Tan
3 Tethera
4 Pethera
5 Pimp
6 Sethera
7 Lethera
8 Hovera
9 Dovera
10 Dick
11 Yan-a-dick
12 Tan-a-dick
13 Tethera-dick
14 Pethera-dick
15 Bumfit
16 Yan-a-bumfit
17 Tan-a-bumfit
18 Tethera-bumfit
19 Pethera-bumfit
20 Jiggit

SILLY FACTS

Easy anagrams

Famous person	Chinston Wurchill
Country	Turkye
Football team	Chesterman Untied
Pop star	Likey Minouge
Animal	Baer
Food	Fish nad chips
Newspaper	The Nus

22 joke shop favourites

1 Stink bombs
2 Itching powder
3 Pepper chewing gum
4 Exploding matches
5 Glow in the dark bogies
6 Disappearing ink
7 Black face soap
8 Hand buzzer
9 Whoopee cushion
10 Fart gas
11 Nail through thumb
12 Plastic doggy-doo
13 Water bombs
14 Plastic vomit
15 Floating eyeball
16 Rubber snake
17 Chilli sweets
18 Loaded dice
19 Chattering teeth
20 Rubber chicken
21 Giant afro wig
22 Fake blood

How to recognise five common trees by the colour of their leaves

Tree	Colour of leaves
Oak	Green
Sycamore	Green
Ash	Green
Birch	Green
Willow	Green

Choccy knowledge

- First year you could buy a bar of choccy: 1847
- Cost of a rabbit in Aztec times: 30 cocoa beans
- Amount of choccy scoffed in the UK each year: 500,000 tonnes
- Cost of 100 g of finest Belgian chocs: £8
- Amount of caffeine in white choccy: none
- Percentage of fat in a choccy bar: 30%

Top geysers

Name	Location	Height of water spout
Loburu	Lake Bogor, Kenya	3 m
Geysers del Tatio	San Pedro de Atacama, Chile	9 m
Pohutu	Rotorua, New Zealand	18 m
The Strokkur	Geysir, Iceland	30 m
Lake Suwa Geyser	Lake Suwa, Japan	35 m
Old Faithful	Yellowstone National Park, USA	50 m
Great Fountain	Yellowstone National Park, USA	60 m
Steamboat Geyser	Yellowstone National Park, USA	90 m

Dodgy mathematical sayings

- There are three kinds of people in the world: those who can count and those who can't
- Algebra was simple for the Romans: X was always 10
- 8/5 of all people do not understand fractions
- The lottery is a tax on people who can't do maths
- Being good with numbers is 90% natural ability and 15% hard work
- The latest survey shows that 1 in 4 people make up 25% of the population

Earthquakes

Richter scale	Effects
3	Small tremors which humans cannot detect
4	Light vibration; hanging objects swing
5	Sleepers awakened; doors swing; liquids spill
6	Difficult for people to stand; windows break; walls crack; bells ring
7	General panic; buildings collapse; landslides happen
8	Rails bent; widespread damage to all buildings; objects thrown into the air

Royal Mint questions and answers

Q. *What does the Royal Mint do?*
A. Makes coins

Q. *How long has it been making coins?*
A. Over 1,100 years

Q. *Who guards the coins?*
A. The Royal Mint has its own mini police force

Q. *Does the Royal Mint only make ordinary coins like 10ps?*
A. No, it makes gold coins, special commemorative coins, blank coins for 100 other countries, medals, awards and tokens

Q. *Does it make bank notes?*
A. No, the Bank of England prints £5, £10, £20 and £50 notes

Q. *Can visitors to the Mint swap their old coins for shiny new ones?*
A. No, people are not allowed to take any coins into the Royal Mint (plastic tokens are used for money)

Best surf

Aveiro	Portugal
Bell's Beach	Victoria, Australia
Croyde Bay	Devon, UK
Hookipa Beach	Hawaii
Jeffreys Bay	South Africa
Metigama	Sri Lanka
Puerto Escondido	Mexico
Teahupoo Beach	Tahiti
Uluwatu	Bali

Top 40 singles containing the word 'moon'

Song	Artist	Chart position	Date
'Sugar Moon'	Pat Boone	6	Jun 1958
'Moon Talk'	Perry Como	17	Sep 1958
'Moon River'	Danny Williams	1	Nov 1961
'Everyone's Gone to the Moon'	Jonathan King	4	Jul 1965
'Walking on the Moon'	The Police	1	Dec 1979
'Bark at the Moon'	Ozzy Osbourne	21	Nov 1983
'Killing Moon'	Echo & The Bunnymen	9	Jan 1984
'Pathway to the Moon'	MN8	25	Feb 1996

Long, long lives

Tortoise	150 years
Human being	120 years
Lobster	100 years
Killer whale	90 years
Golden eagle	80 years
Elephant	77 years
Ostrich	62 years
Stinkpot	53½ years

Slang

Jim-jams	Pyjamas
Road apple	Horse manure in the streets
Wake	Short for 'way cool'
Chunter	To complain or mutter
Blob wagon	Ambulance
Kibosh	To put the kibosh on something means to ruin it
Phat	Excellent
Honcho	Boss
Clag	Bad weather

Sumo moves

Oshi-dashi	The push-out
Yori-kiri	The force-out
Hataki-komi	The dodge and slap down
Sukui nage	The scoop throw
Tsuri-otoshi	The lift and smash down
Uchi-gake	The inner leg trip
Abise-taoshi	The chest lunge

Firsts

Hamburger	USA	1889
Fireworks	China	1103
Vaulting horse	Sweden	1761
Jeans	USA	1850
Blindfold chess match	Italy	1266
Laxative	Germany	1625
Windscreen wipers	UK	1921
Stuffed birds	Holland	1517
Lottery	Belgium	1446

Old things

Old Bailey	The Central Criminal Court in London
Old Bill	The police
Old King Cole	A merry old soul
Old Master	A painting by a great artist of the 13th-17th centuries
Old Nick	The devil
Old school	Old fashioned
Old wives' tale	A superstition
Old man of Hoy	A 137 m high column of rock in the Orkney Islands
Old bean	Same as old fellow, old chap, old fruit and old thing

Seven words for head

1 Bonce
2 Noggin
3 Pate
4 Brain
5 Skull
6 Nut
7 Noodle

SILLY FACTS

Essential knowledge

What's got two humps and is found on Jupiter?	A very lost camel
What's blue and ticks?	A clockwork nun
What's yellow and white and travels at 225 km/h (140 mph)?	A train driver's egg sandwich
What's got two taps and an aerial?	A radio-controlled bidet
What looks like half a pineapple?	The other half
What is heavier in summer than in winter?	Traffic to the beach
What's hot and good at climbing hills?	A four-wheel drive curry

Major feats in minor cricket

Fastest century	22 balls by Don Bradman, 1931
Most sixes off successive balls	9 by Jim Smith, 1935
Most runs off one stroke	11 by Philip Mitford, 1903
Highest individual innings	628 by Arthur Collins, 1899
Longest time at crease without scoring	100 minutes by Ian Balfour, 1963
Best bowling figures	10 wickets for 0 runs by Jennings Tune, 1922

Seven miracles of Jesus

- Turning water into wine
- Calming a storm
- Feeding 5,000 people
- Walking on the sea
- Healing a blind man
- Causing a huge catch of fish
- Raising Lazarus from the dead

Number of Olympic Games' competitors

1896 Athens	311
1904 St Louis	625
1924 Paris	3,092
1960 Rome	5,348
1988 Seoul	8,465
2000 Sydney	10,651

Eight computer viruses

Name	Type
Ripper	Disk write corruption
Southghost	Worm
Tinydog	Backdoor trojan horse
Feast	Polymorphic PHP
Killerwhale.713	Memory resident
X97M.sugar	Excel macro
Ping Pong	DOS
Outback steakhouse	Hoax

Nine geniuses

1 Archimedes (mathematician & inventor), born 287 BC
2 Leonardo da Vinci (artist, inventor and more), born 1452
3 Galileo (astronomer & philosopher), born 1564
4 Rembrandt (painter), born 1606
5 Isaac Newton (scientist & mathematician), born 1642
6 Mozart (composer), born 1756
7 Thomas Edison (inventor), born 1847
8 Marie Curie (scientist), born 1867
9 Albert Einstein (scientist), born 1879

The most densely and least densely populated countries

Country	People per sq km
Monaco	16,300
Singapore	6,600
Malta	1,200
Maldives	1,000
Bahrain	900
Mauritania	2.7
Suriname	2.7
Australia	2.5
Namibia	2.2
Mongolia	1.7

Intriguing animals

Shrew	Has poisonous spit
Lion	A major snoozer – sleeps for up to 20 hours a day
Chameleon	Its tongue is almost as long as its body
Blue whales	Have big, big babies, weighing about 5 tonnes
Cuckoo	The only bird that can eat the woolly bear caterpillar
Black bean aphids	Fight off ladybird larvae by kicking them
Catfish	Can grow to 5 m long in some European lakes
Starfish	If cut in two, both halves will grow into starfish

Buckingham Palace has its own...

Post office
Police station
Doctor
Fire brigade
Chapel
Electricians, plumbers and carpenters
Laundry
Bar

Nine US candy bars

- 3 Musketeers
- Baby Ruth
- Strawberry Charleston Chew
- Peanut Butter Cookie Dough Bites
- Graham Flipz
- Hershey Hugs
- Reese's Nutrageous
- Tootsie Pops
- Whatchamacallit

A few of the muscles in your body

Extensor digitorum	Arm
Sartorius	Leg
Occipitofrontalis	Head
Sternocleidomastoid	Neck
Gluteus maximus	Bum
Psoas	Torso
Flexor digiti minimi	Foot

Wacky chemical substances

Unununium	Element number 111
Cummingtonite	A mineral found in America
Moronic acid	An acid found in resin
Curious chloride	A radioactive compound
Arabitol	A type of alcohol (not made from bunnies)
Commic acid	A chemical made from myrrh trees
Gardinin	Yellow crystals made from plants
Antipain	A poisonous compound
Penguinone	Real name: 3,4,4,5-tetramethylcyclohexa-2,5-dienone

Six classic spoonerisms

1 You have hissed my mystery lecture
2 Three cheers for the queer old dean
3 You have tasted two worms
4 Our Lord is a shoving leopard
5 It is kisstomary to cuss the bride
6 A well-boiled icicle

Things you can wind up

An old clock
A ball of string
A fishing reel
A clockwork mouse
A capstan
A gramophone
Your sister

11 slightly rude or silly UK place names

1	Hairy Side	Northumberland
2	Boghead	Aberdeenshire
3	Wetwang	East Yorkshire
4	Nasty	Hertfordshire
5	Booby Dingle	Herefordshire
6	Ugley	Essex
7	Nether Wallop	Hampshire
8	Panty Hill	Powys
9	Great Cockup	Cumbria
10	Fartown	Kirklees
11	Burnt Bottom	Dorset

Ten colourful birds

1 Blue-footed booby
2 Black-necked screamer
3 Crimson-rumped waxbill
4 White-bearded honeyeater
5 Yellow-bellied sapsucker
6 Green glistening tanager
7 Golden-rumped tinker bird
8 Red-billed oxpecker
9 Grey-sided laughing thrush
10 Purple grackle

Big UK tourist attractions in 2001

Attraction	No. of visitors
Blackpool Pleasure Beach	6.5m
The British Museum	4.6m
Tate Modern	3.6m
York Minster	1.6m
Legoland Windsor	1.6m
Edinburgh Castle	1.1m

Hal|ves

Half-baked	Daft
Half board	Accommodation with breakfast and evening meal
Half-butt	An extra long snooker cue
Half-crown	An old coin worth 12½p
Half-hardy	A plant that can survive most cold weather
Half-hearted	Lacking enthusiasm
Half-light	Gloomy light at dawn or dusk
Half-nelson	A wrestling hold
Halfpenny	An old coin worth, well, half a penny
Half-pipe	A u-shaped structure used by skaters and snowboarders
Half-timbered	Building with a wooden frame filled with other materials
Half-track	A vehicle with caterpillar tracks and wheels
Half-volley	When a ball is struck on the bounce
Halfwit	Someone who's not too clever

Whopping soccer transfer fees

Player	Club	Amount
Juan Veron	Lazio to Man Utd (2001)	£28.1m
Ronaldo	Inter Milan to Real Madrid (2002)	£28.5m
Gaizka Mendicta	Valencia to Lazio (2001)	£29m
Rio Ferdinand	Leeds Utd to Man Utd (2002)	£29.1m
Christian Vieri	Lazio to Inter Milan (1999)	£32m
Gianluigi Buffon	Parma to Juventus (2001)	£32.6m
Hernan Crespo	Parma to Lazio (2000)	£35.5m
Luis Figo	Barcelona to Real Madrid (2000)	£37m
Zinedine Zidane	Juventus to Real Madrid (2001)	£45.6m

Four words with no rhymes

• Orange • Month • Silver • Purple

Beanie Baby reptiles

Ally the alligator
Hissy the snake
Iggy the iguana
Lizzy the lizard
Peekaboo the turtle
Snake the snake
Scaly the lizard
Slither the snake
Speedy the turtle
Zoom the turtle

13 *Star Wars* characters and beasties

1 Tusken raiders
2 Jawas
3 Krayt dragon
4 Droids
5 Swamp slug
6 Tauntauns
7 Wampa ice creatures
8 Space slugs
9 Mynocks
10 Ewoks
11 Yuzzums
12 Blurrgs
13 Thrantras

Fabled fiends of ancient Greece

Name	Appearance	Dirty deeds
Argus	Big ugly man with 100 eyes	Bouncer for Zeus' mistresses; good lookout
Centaurs	Half men, half-horse	Savage kidnappers of brides; expensive in hay
Hydra	Snake monster with nine heads	Used poisonous breath and head replacement powers to make mincemeat of victims, except Hercules
Sirens	Birds with women's heads	Lured sailors on to deadly rocks with their mesmerising voices. Just ignore them
Cerberus	Three-headed guard dog	Stopped innocent people going in and out of the underworld; not interested in 'walkies'
Gorgons	Women with hair full of snakes	Their gaze turned people to stone; conversation limited
Scylla	Overlarge monster with six dog heads around her waist	Ate anything and everything that came near. Not to be confused with Scylla Black

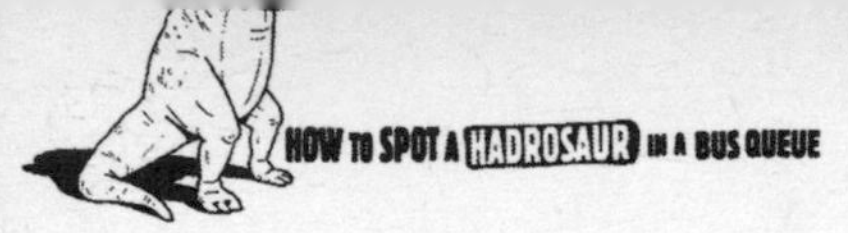

Three strange years

45 BC

This 'Year of Confusion' was 445 days long because the Romans added an extra 80 days to correct previous mistakes in the calendar

1582

In many countries the dates 5-14th October were removed from the year to adjust Julius Caesar's calendar (which had overestimated the length of a year). Bad news if your birthday was then...

1752

11 days were taken off this year in Britain, making September only 19 days long. People who went to sleep on the evening of 2nd September woke up on the 14th, causing riots and demands for the government to 'Give us our 11 days back!'

Six things glue can be made from

• Bones • Hooves • Animal skin
• Milk • Blood • Plants

Seven doubtful crisp flavours

1 Sprout & liver
2 Prune cocktail
3 Smokey lard
4 Cheese & donkey
5 Roast lettuce
6 Earwax & vinegar
7 Cabbage & toenail

The Humber Bridge

Length of cable	71,000 km
Amount of steel	27,500 tonnes
Amount of concrete	480,000 tonnes
Thickness of main cables	68 cm
Number of wires in each cable	14,948
Total length of bridge	2,220 m
Max depth of foundations	36 m
Height of towers	155.5 m

Ten characters from *Tom & Jerry*

1 Tom (cat)
2 Jerry (mouse)
3 Spike (dog)
4 Mammy Two-shoes (human)
5 Nibbles (mouse)
6 Butch (cat)
7 Meathead (cat)
8 Quacker (duckling)
9 Toodles (cat)
10 Tyke (puppy)

Average life expectancy in 2003

Japan	81 years
UK	78 years
Russia	68 years
Cambodia	58 years
South Africa	47 years
Mozambique	31 years

SILLY FACTS

Nine inventions with limited potential

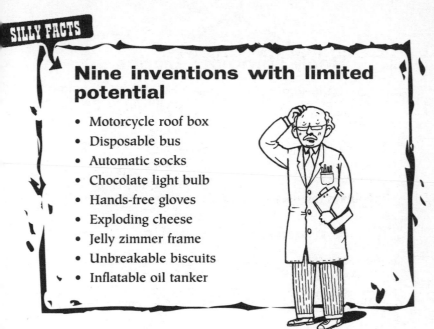

- Motorcycle roof box
- Disposable bus
- Automatic socks
- Chocolate light bulb
- Hands-free gloves
- Exploding cheese
- Jelly zimmer frame
- Unbreakable biscuits
- Inflatable oil tanker

Comet tales

- Halley's Comet has a tail 6,000,000 km long
- Comets sometimes travel tail-first
- Some comets lose 300 million tonnes of material during each journey back to the Sun
- In 1846 Biela's Comet split in two
- There is a comet orbiting between Saturn and Jupiter called Schwassman-Wachmann 1
- West's Comet, seen in 1976, will next be seen in the year 559000

Rock climbing grades

Difficult	Hard, very severe
Very difficult	Extreme 1
Severe	Extreme 2
Hard severe	Extreme 3
Very severe	

A number of books

One Hundred and One Dalmatians	Dodie Smith, 1956
Two Weeks with The Queen	Morris Gleitzman, 1989
Three Men in a Boat	Jerome K. Jerome, 1889
Four Friends Together	Sue Heap, 2004
Five Go Down to the Sea	Enid Blyton, 1953
Six Dinner Sid	Inga Moore, 1990
Seven Ways to Catch the Moon	M.P. Robertson, 2000
Eight Days of Luke	Diana Wynne Jones, 1985
Nine Lives of Montezuma	Michael Morpurgo, 2002
Ten Hours to Live	Pete Johnson, 1995

Big, medium and small coffee drinkers

Country	Kg per person per year
Finland	11.3
Sweden	9.7
France	5.5
UK	2.8
Syria	1
Peru	0.2
North Korea	0

Stupid signs

DO NOT READ THIS SIGN

OPEN
7 DAYS
A WEEK
Except Tuesdays

250

NO
SHOPLIFTING
It's far too heavy

THE FARMER ALLOWS WALKERS TO CROSS THIS FIELD FOR FREE BUT THE BULL CHARGES

IF YOU CANNOT READ – LEARN HERE

Banana knowledge

Leaves	Banana leaves grow up to 4 m long
Types	These include red bananas, apple-bananas, baby-bananas and baking bananas
Drink	In East Africa you can buy banana beer
Fruit?	In some countries green bananas are cooked and eaten as vegetables
Vitamins	Bananas are the only fruit to contain all the major vitamins
Hungry?	Australia grows over 1/4 million tonnes of bananas each year
Bunches	Bananas grow upwards in bunches called hands
Gassy	Bananas give off ethylene, a flammable gas which causes them to ripen

Eight paintings with long titles

1	Rembrandt	*Saskia van Uylenburgh in Arcadian Costume*
2	Jan Steen	*A Man Blowing Smoke at a Drunken Woman*
3	Jacob Maris	*A Windmill and Houses beside Water: Stormy Sky*
4	Jan Weenix	*A Huntsman Cutting up a Dead Deer, with Two Deerhounds*
5	Leonardo da Vinci	*The Virgin and Child with Saint Anne and Saint John the Baptist*
6	J.M.W. Turner	*Sun Rising Through Vapour: Fisherman Cleaning and Selling Fish*
7	Canaletto	*Venice: the Upper Reaches of the Grand Canal with S. Simon Piccolo*
8	J.M.W. Turner	*A River with a Mill and Two-Arched Bridge above a Weir, with a Classical Church (?or Villa) on the Far Bank beneath a High Cliff*

Sums that nearly add up to 9

$4\frac{1}{2} + 4$

$9 + 0.00002$

$27001 \div 3000$

1.7×5.3

$7787 - 7777$

Exciting football matches

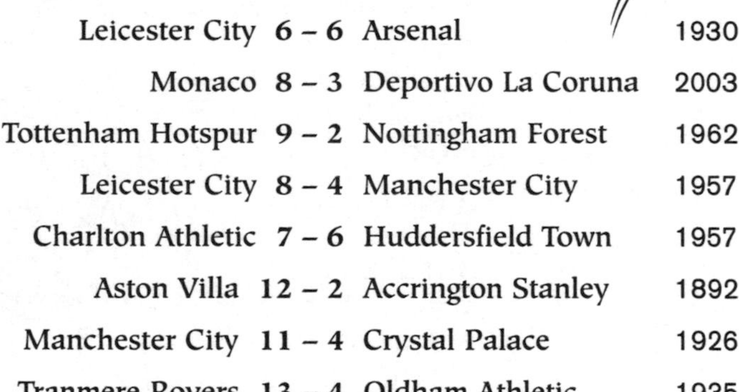

Leicester City	6 – 6	Arsenal	1930
Monaco	8 – 3	Deportivo La Coruna	2003
Tottenham Hotspur	9 – 2	Nottingham Forest	1962
Leicester City	8 – 4	Manchester City	1957
Charlton Athletic	7 – 6	Huddersfield Town	1957
Aston Villa	12 – 2	Accrington Stanley	1892
Manchester City	11 – 4	Crystal Palace	1926
Tranmere Rovers	13 – 4	Oldham Athletic	1935

The magnificent Munros (the highest peaks in Scotland)

1	Ben Nevis	1,344 m	4,409 ft
2	Ben Macdui	1,309 m	4,295 ft
3	Braeriach	1,296 m	4,252 ft
4	Cairn Toul	1,291 m	4,236 ft
5	Sgor an Lochain Uaine	1,258 m	4,127 ft
6	Cairngorm	1,244 m	4,081 ft
7	Aonach Beag	1,234 m	4,049 ft
8	Aonach Mor	1,221 m	4,006 ft
9	Carn Mor Deag	1,220 m	4,003 ft

The only six kings of Belgium

1	Leopold I	1831-1865
2	Leopold II	1865-1909
3	Albert I	1909-1934
4	Leopold III	1934-1951
5	Baudouin I	1951-1993
6	Albert II	1993-

SILLY FACTS

What do you call a man with...

a paper bag on his head?	Russell
a spade on his head?	Doug
a car on his head?	Jack
a kilt on his head?	Scott
a lion on his head?	Claude
a toilet on his head?	Lou
a legal document on his head?	Will
a car number plate on his head?	Reg
a rabbit on his head?	Warren
a coat on his head?	Mac
a casserole on his head?	Stu
a trampoline on his head?	Jim
half a drum on his head?	Tom
a man on his head?	Guy
a bus on his head?	The deceased

Who was beheaded?

Anne Boleyn	1536
Catherine Howard	1542
Lady Jane Grey	1554
Mary Queen of Scots	1587
Earl of Essex	1601
Sir Walter Raleigh	1618
Charles I	1649

Baked bean expertise

- 6th January is National Bean Day in America
- Australian cricketer Shane Warne is a baked bean addict
- In Britain each person eats about 7 kg of baked beans every year
- Heinz Baked Beans have been going since 1895
- 1.2 million cans of beans are scoffed each week in the UK
- In the early 1900s, baked beans were marketed as a luxury food
- Baked beans contain sugars which cause gas in the human digestive system – but you already knew that...

Nine incorrect spellings ✗ of 'necessary'

1 neccesary
2 neseccary
3 nessesary
4 nescesary
5 necessery
6 necassary
7 nececcery
8 nesecary
9 mangle

Christmas snippets

- In AD 200 in Egypt, Christmas was celebrated on 20th May
- For centuries Christmas Day in England was 5th January
- Ukranian churches celebrate Christmas on 7th January
- Christmas was forbidden by an Act of Parliament in 1644
- Belgium removed 10 days from its calendar on 21st December 1582; consequently there was no Christmas Day that year
- In many European countries, presents are opened on Christmas Eve

14 human parasites

	Parasite	Where they live	Typical size
1	Head lice	Hair	3 mm
2	Body lice	Clothes	4 mm
3	Scabies mites	Skin	0.05 mm
4	Human fleas	Clothes, skin	3 mm
5	Pinworms	Intestine	1 cm
6	Hookworms	Skin, lungs, intestine	1 cm
7	Guinea worms	Intestine, skin	1 metre
8	Tapeworms	Intestine	2 metres
9	Flukes	Liver	0.1 mm
10	Chiggers	Armpits	6 mm
11	Bedbugs	Beds	8 mm
12	Bot fly larvae	Head	25 mm
13	Congo floor maggots	Skin	3 mm
14	Leeches	Skin, throat, nose	3 cm

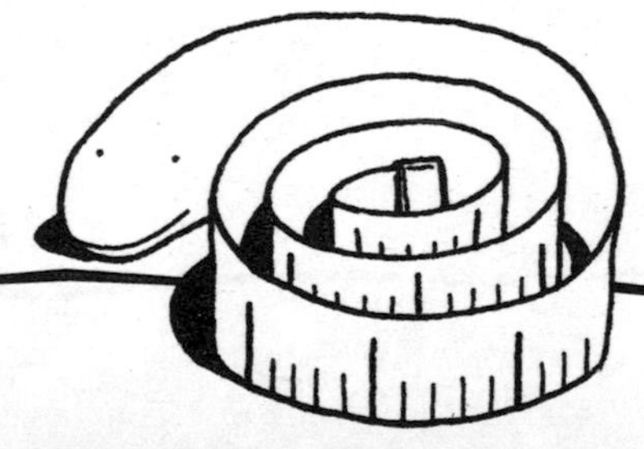

Beetle behaviour

Great diving beetle	Eats small fish
Histerid beetle	Lives in cow dung
Bladder beetle	Female bites male before mating
Sexton beetle	Buries dead animals to lay eggs on
Goldsmith	Eats snails
Devil's coach horse	Hunts maggots
Oil beetle	Larvae attach themselves to bees
Furniture beetle	Eats wooden furniture
Glow worm	Signals to mate with luminous body
Cardinal beetle	Larvae are cannibals
Click beetle	Uses a self-righting mechanism if tipped over
Dor beetle	Eats human poo

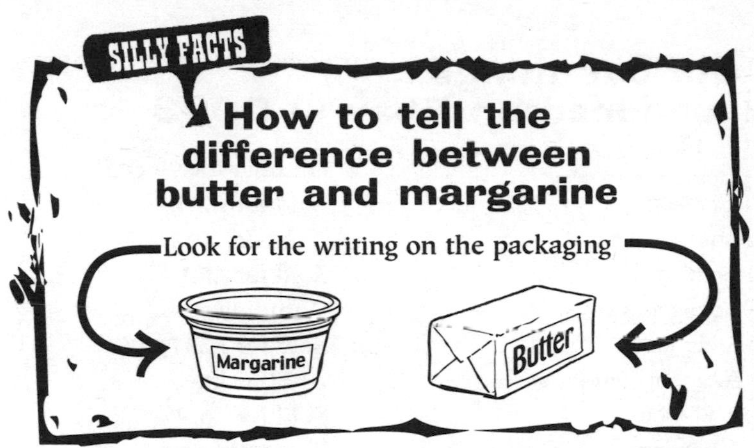

SILLY FACTS
How to tell the difference between butter and margarine
Look for the writing on the packaging
Margarine
Butter

The former names of countries

Current name	Old name
Ethiopia	Abyssinia
Mali	French Sudan
Tonga	Friendly Islands
Ghana	Gold Coast
Zimbabwe	Southern Rhodesia
Democratic Republic of Congo	Zaire
Sri Lanka	Ceylon
Bangladesh	East Pakistan
Iran	Persia
Myanmar	Burma
Indonesia	Dutch East Indies
Thailand	Siam

Curious things auctioned on Ebay in 2003

Iraq	On offer for 99 cents
2p piece	Sold for £7.50
Aberystwyth	'Sold' for £22
Nothing	Sold for £50
Someone's wife	Withdrawn
A big ferry	Sold for £237,000
A bag of conkers	£4.50 wanted
A £5 note	Sold for £6.99
A banana	Bids unknown
Sunday League football team Dynamo Kebab	Sold for £31

SILLY FACTS

Seven people to be wary of

1 A blind surgeon
2 A vegetarian butcher
3 A toddler with a pickaxe
4 A grumpy dentist
5 A policeman wearing a leotard
6 A learner tank driver
7 A human guinea pig

12 kites

1. Blue Hill meteorological box kite
2. Hakkaku kite
3. Bermudan three-stick
4. Thai serpent
5. French pear top
6. Chinese rice kite
7. Korean fighter
8. Brazilian bird
9. Cody's war kite
10. Double rhomboidal compound kite
11. Bell's multi-celled tetrahedral kite
12. Marconi-rigged jib kite

Beckham's haircuts

1991	Centre parting
1996	Brylcreem slickback
1998	Bleached curtains
2000	Grade 1 shave
2001	Short back and sides
2001	Mohawk
2002	Lion's mane
2002	Blond bedhead
2003	Braided corn rows
2003	Alice band
2004	Spanish pony tail
2004	Close crew cut

Snow

- Snowflakes each contain a particle of dust
- Snowflakes all have six sides
- Snow is transparent – it only appears white because the ice crystals in it reflect light
- Snow is a good insulator of heat
- Snowflakes are sometimes 10 cm in diameter – the largest ever was 38 cm
- Snow is sometimes pink if it mixes with red dust in the air
- Snow 20 cm deep contains the same amount of water as about 2 cm of rain
- Snowfalls can be heavy in Alaska – in 1955 over $1\frac{1}{2}$ metres of snow fell in a single day

Food and drink in Polish

Bread	Chleb
Fish	Ryby
Soup	Zupa
Carp	Karp
Bacon	Bekon boczek
Wild boar	Dzik
Peas	Groch
Raspberries	Maliny
Ice cream	Lody
Beer	Piwo
Wine	Wino
Beetroot soup	Barszcz czerwony

The fates of James Bond villains

Villain	Film	Fate
Oddjob	*Goldfinger*	Electrocuted by James Bond
Dr No	*Dr No*	Falls into a radioactive pool
Hugo Drax	*Moonraker*	Injected with a poisoned dart and shot into space
Max Zorin	*A View to a Kill*	Falls off the Golden Gate bridge
Blofeld	*Diamonds are Forever*	Gets away
Goldfinger	*Goldfinger*	Sucked out of a decompressed aircraft
Elliot Carver	*Tomorrow Never Dies*	Mangled by a giant tunnelling sea drill
Scaramanga	*The Man with the Golden Gun*	Shot by Bond in a duel
Jaws	*The Spy Who Loved Me*	Bond lets him go after he turns nice
Mr Big	*Live and Let Die*	Explodes after eating a special compressed air pellet

Elizabethan con-men and swindlers

Tom o' Bedlams	Thieves who wore fox tails and pretended to be mad
Rufflers	Beggars who claimed to be wounded soldiers
Dommerars	Men who pretended to be mutes (unable to speak)
Clapperdogeons	Beggars who used children to gain sympathy
Prancers	Horse thieves who carried saddles for a quick getaway
Strowling Morts	Old women acting as widows to beg
Anglers	Robbers who stole from open windows using fishing rods and hooks
Whip Jack	A sailor who begged with a 'shipwrecked woman'

11 things you couldn't get 20 years ago

1. A *Fimbles* video
2. Golden Grahams
3. Hotmail
4. A Beckham shirt
5. Sky
6. An MP3 player
7. UK National Lottery tickets
8. A Peugeot 206
9. A holiday in Croatia
10. Wakeboard lessons
11. A king-sized Snickers

Eight theatre superstitions

1. Never say, 'Macbeth'
2. Never whistle in the dressing room
3. Never knit in the wings
4. Never use real flowers on stage
5. It's unlucky to say, 'Good Luck', to an actor, but lucky to say, 'Break a leg'
6. It's unlucky to wear green in a play
7. It's unlucky for a visitor to enter a dressing room with the left foot first
8. Peacock feathers are a no-no

Words that rhyme with 'moo' but don't look like 'moo'

Do	Queue	Flu	Ewe
Two	Through	Pooh	You
Glue	View	Roux	Lieu
Few	Coup	Shoe	Gnu

King Zog

- Zog was king of Albania from 1928-1939
- His real name was Ahmed Bey Zogu
- Zog was Prime Minister and President of Albania before declaring himself king
- He was a Muslim
- King Zog was also known as Skanderbeg III
- During World War II, Ian Fleming (author of the *James Bond* novels) helped Zog to escape to Britain
- In Britain, Zog stayed at The Ritz Hotel in London, arriving with suitcases containing gold
- His wedding cake was 3 metres wide
- Zog was an unpopular king in Albania
- He survived 55 assassination attempts
- Zog died in France in 1961

Who grows the most spuds?

Country	Tonnes per year
China	58,000,000
Poland	23,000,000
Germany	12,000,000
UK	7,000,000
Italy	2,000,000
Jamaica	8,000
Bahrain	16

Nine WWE wrestlers

1 Blue Meanie
2 The Rock
3 Triple H
4 Crash Holly
5 Perry Saturn
6 Stone Cold Steve Austin
7 Tazz
8 The Undertaker
9 Scotty 2 Hotty

SILLY FACTS

Seven lies about Rhyl

1. Rhyl is the capital of Spain
2. The older parts of Rhyl are constructed from pasta
3. Friday in Rhyl is called Tuesday, and Tuesday is called Desmond
4. In Rhyl, soup is against the law
5. Anyone in Rhyl over the age of 63 must wear two hats
6. Rhyl is closed in October
7. To save money, many Rhyl families share one very large shoe

12 things that change colour

1. Traffic lights
2. Chameleons
3. Autumn leaves
4. Bananas
5. Embarrassed cheeks
6. Toasted bread
7. Weasels
8. The Iron Man's eyes
9. Bunsen burner flame
10. Sunset skies
11. Hair
12. Litmus paper

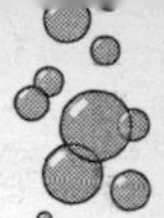

Ten American towns

Correctionville (Iowa)	Riddle (Oregon)
Newcomerstown (Ohio)	Twitty (Texas)
Bad Axe (Michigan)	Plain Dealing (Louisiana)
Cannon Ball (N. Dakota)	Climax (Georgia)
Surprise (Nebraska)	Zap (N. Dakota)

Bubblewrap

- Invented: 1950s
- What it is: cushioned packaging material
- Who makes it: Sealed Air Corporation, amongst others
- Colours: transparent, and pink for anti-static bubblewrap
- How it's made: it's a secret...
- Other uses: keeping drinks cool, greenhouse insulation, clothes for clubbers, popping
- Popping methods: thumb-press, finger-squeeze, fist-whack, wring-twist, floor-jump
- Mean trick: hide bubblewrap under a doormat on a hard floor
- Pop virtual bubblewrap: at www.virtual-bubblewrap.com

Ten words beginning with 'O'

Oche	The line you throw from in darts
Ocotillo	A spiny hedge plant
Odd-toed ungulate	A type of mammal including horses and rhinos
Ogdoad	Eight of something
Oldster	An old person
Ollycrock	A type of shellfish
Onkus	Yucky
Oodles	A large amount
Oojamaflip	Something you've forgotten the name of
Oubliette	A secret dungeon with a trap door entrance

How to spot a hadrosaur in a bus queue

Hadrosaur

Fanzines

Sport	Team	Fanzine
Baseball	Various	*Zisk*
Football	Chester City	*Hello Albert*
Ice Hockey	Sheffield Shadows	*The Sha Doh!*
Rugby League	Warrington	*House of Pain*
Football	Hamilton Academicals	*Crying Time Again*
Cricket	Surrey	*Who's Surrey Now?*
Football	Middlesbrough	*Fly Me to the Moon*
Rugby League	Salford	*The Scarlet Turkey*
Speedway	Newcastle	*Diamonds are Forever*

15 ~~miztakes~~ mistakes

1. Error
2. Gaffe
3. No-no
4. Whoopsie
5. Oversight
6. Clanger
7. Howler
8. Slip
9. Bad idea
10. Blunder
11. Botch
12. Bungle
13. Bloomer
14. Blot
15. Boob

Women inventors

Mary Anderson	Windscreen wipers
Bette Graham	Liquid paper
Josephine Cochran	Dishwasher
Stephanie Kwolek	Kevlar
Lillian Gilbreth	Electric food mixer
Randi Altschul	Disposable cell phone
Ruth Handler	Barbie Doll

SILLY FACTS

Unusual hobbies for fish

- Carpentry
- Collecting china teapots
- Playing snooker
- Recreating the major battles of the Boer War
- Knitting

20 ricochet words

Pell-mell
Riff-raff
Hoity-toity
Mish-mash
Hocus-pocus
Tip-top
Hanky-panky
Pitter-patter
Willy-nilly
Helter-skelter
Airy-fairy
Harum-scarum
Fuddy-duddy
Argy-bargy
Razzle-dazzle
Hurly-burly
Tittle-tattle
Namby-pamby
Ding-dong
Flip-flop

SILLY FACTS

Top five causes of broken biscuits

1. Dropping on floor
2. Snapping on purpose
3. Using packet to hammer in fence post
4. Major earthquake
5. Use of axe to open wrapper

Ten less common boys' names and their meanings

Alfonso	Warrior
Baldwin	Brave friend
Cadwallader	Battle chief
Clovis	Warrior
Cosmo	Order
Gaspar	(It has no meaning)
Horace	Roman clan name
Peregrine	Traveller
Torquil	A Norwegian name
Ulick	After Ulysses, the Greek hero

Nine skateboard tricks

1 Nollie
2 Pop shove-it
3 Boneless
4 Blunt fakie
5 Old school kickflip
6 Roast beef
7 Melon
8 180 Hand plant powerslide
9 Pretzel plant

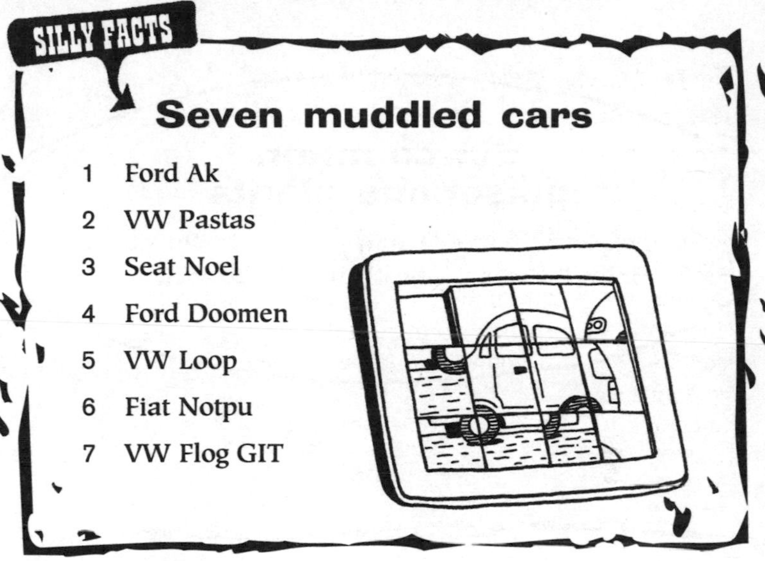

Seven muddled cars

1 Ford Ak

2 VW Pastas

3 Seat Noel

4 Ford Doomen

5 VW Loop

6 Fiat Notpu

7 VW Flog GIT

Six household hints about colds from 1880

1 Wear cork soles in your boots

2 Let children's petticoats be a good way over their knees

3 High-necked frocks are a necessity for little ones

4 Beware of fog

5 Paste brown paper inside worn shoes

6 Light a fire in a foggy bedroom

Six common poisonous plants

1 Foxglove
2 Holly
3 Lupin
4 Mistletoe
5 Privet
6 Yew

Men's high jump world record

Year	Height
1912	2.00 m
1933	2.04 m
1941	2.10 m
1960	2.22 m
1973	2.30 m
1980	2.35 m
1985	2.40 m
1993	2.45 m

16 red things

Red Cross	An emergency relief organisation that helps people during disasters or wars
Red flag	A sign of danger
Red herring	A false clue
Red-letter day	A lucky day
Red rag (to a bull)	Something that greatly angers someone
Red Sea	Sea between Egypt and Arabia crossed by Moses
Red tape	A mass of rules and regulations
Red-handed	Caught red-handed means caught in the act of doing something wrong
Redneck	An American term for a simple country person
Red Admiral	A type of butterfly
Red carpet	A special strip of carpet laid out for royalty or other VIPs
Red dwarf	An old small star which has cooled down
Red rose	The symbol of the county of Lancashire
Red Square	A large open space in Moscow, Russia
Redwood	The tallest tree in the world
Red card	A card used by football referees to send off players

12 rulers

1	King	5	Duke	9	Pharaoh
2	Sultan	6	Lord	10	Queen
3	Emperor	7	Prince	11	Shah
4	Czar	8	Maharajah	12	Sultan

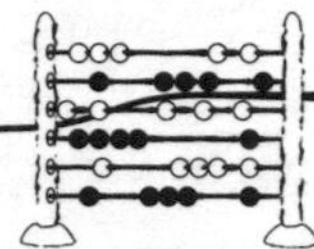

BIG numbers

1,000,000 (10^6)	Million
1,000,000,000 (10^9)	Billion
1,000,000,000,000 (10^{12})	Trillion
1,000,000,000,000,000 (10^{15})	Quadrillion
(10^{18})	Quintillion
(10^{21})	Sextillion
(10^{24})	Septillion
(10^{27})	Octillion
(10^{30})	Nonillion
(10^{33})	Decillion
(10^{63})	Vigintillion

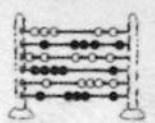

SILLY FACTS

Crimes committed by Goldilocks

- Trespass
- Breaking and entering
- Theft
- Destruction of property

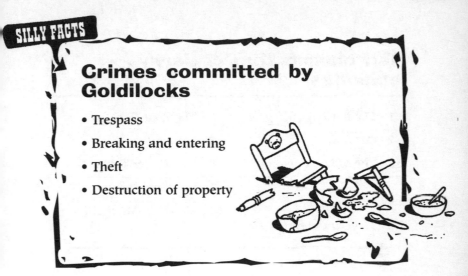

Nine new sports

1 Mountain Unicycling
2 Extreme Ironing
3 Street Luge
4 Wheelbarrow Freestyle
5 Sky Surfing
6 Urban Housework
7 Extreme Croquet
8 Helibungee
9 Zorb

Ten classic *Tom & Jerry* episodes

1 *The Bowling Alley Cat*
2 *Cat Fishin'*
3 *The Mouse Comes to Dinner*
4 *Professor Tom*
5 *The Cat Concerto*
6 *The Zoot Cat*
7 *Tee for Two*
8 *Salt Water Tabby*
9 *Jerry and Jumbo*
10 *Mouse in Manhattan*

17 types of nonsense

1 Poppycock
2 Twaddle
3 Tosh
4 Blather
5 Rot
6 Gibberish
7 Balderdash
8 Bosh
9 Tripe
10 Piffle
11 Hogwash
12 Bilge
13 Claptrap
14 Drivel
15 Bunkum
16 Humbug
17 Boloney

SILLY FACTS

Six things not to wear at a wedding

1 Wellies
2 Fake ears
3 A crash helmet
4 More than four pairs of underpants
5 The bride's dress (unless you're the bride)
6 Armour

Six satellites of Uranus

• Juliet • Puck • Desdemona
• Bianca • Rosalind • Ariel

Provisions taken on board Captain Cook's ship *The Resolution* for his second great voyage in 1772

28,000 kg of ship's biscuits
14 tonnes of salt beef
27 tonnes of salt pork
1,400 kg of raisins
19 tonnes of beer
2,900 litres of wine
9 tonnes of sauerkraut (pickled cabbage)
135 litres of carrot marmalade

Seven places in Australia with Aboriginal names

1. Bindebango
2. Boongoondoo
3. Goondiwindi
4. Boggabilla
5. Lake Kittakittaooloo
6. Wagga Wagga
7. Lake Cadibarrawirracanna

Number of mobile phones in the UK

1982	10,000
1991	1 million
1993	2 million
1995	5 million
1999	24 million
2001	40 million
2004	50 million

Mountain rescue code

Red Flare	SOS
White Flare	Message understood
Green Flare	Return to base

SILLY FACTS

Eight people you can eat

1 Mr Bean
2 Mark Fish
3 Jasper Carrott
4 Massimo Maccarone
5 Tim Rice
6 Kevin Bacon
7 Albert R. Broccoli
8 Patrick Berger

Six Geordie words

1	Rozzle	To heat over a fire
2	Dunt	To hit someone's bottom
3	Ken	To know
4	Lavvy	Toilet
5	Muggles	Marbles
6	Banky	Steep

Seven nasty, nasty ~~spelins~~ ~~spelings~~ spellings

1 Catarrh
2 Fluorescent
3 Manoeuvre
4 Diarrhoea
5 Sergeant
6 Unnecessary
7 Weird

Ten bottled beers

1 Goose Eye Wonkey Donkey (Goose Eye Brewery)
2 Fire-Bellied Toad (Frog Island Brewery)
3 La'al Cockle Warmer (Jenning's Brewery)
4 Kamikaze (Dent Brewery)
5 Black Dog (Elwood's Brewery)
6 Old Growler (Nethergate Brewery)
7 Head Cracker (Woodforde's Brewery)
8 Old Slug Porter (RCH Brewery)
9 Piddle in the Hole (Wyre Piddle Brewery)
10 Old Fart (Merriman's Brewery)

Women's world record marathon times

1926	3h 40m
1964	3h 27m
1967	3h 07m
1971	2h 46m
1980	2h 25m
1999	2h 20m
2003	2h 15m

Wallace & Gromit gems

- Gromit is 11 cm tall
- *A Grand Day Out* took 6 years to make
- The music for *A Close Shave* was provided by a 65-piece orchestra
- Nick Park, the creator of *Wallace & Gromit*, has won three Oscars
- About £50 million worth of W & G merchandise is sold each year
- Wallace lives at 62 West Wallaby Street
- Preston the dog's favourite newspaper is 'The Daily Telegruff'

The number of times some words appear in the Bible

Bucket	1
Wolf	6
Belly	9
Ziz	1
Spattered	3
Toes	8
Baboons	2
Pomegranates	24
Baldhead	2
The	55,728

16 monsters

1 Banshee
2 King Kong
3 Roc
4 Harpy
5 Bigfoot
6 Werewolf
7 Godzilla
8 Nessie
9 Leviathan
10 Minotaur
11 Kraken
12 Cyclops
13 Phoenix
14 Medusa
15 Grendel
16 Dragon

11 chasing games

1 Tag
2 British Bulldog
3 Capture the Flag
4 Darebase
5 Duck Duck Goose
6 Kick the Can
7 Kings and Queens
8 Octopus Tag
9 Pickle
10 Prisoner's Base
11 What's the Time Mr Wolf?

Four seas of the moon

- Sea of Tranquillity
- Sea of Showers
- Ocean of Storms
- Bay of Rainbows

Ten old kids' TV programmes

1. *Animal Magic*
2. *Bananaman*
3. *Bod*
4. *Crackerjack*
5. *Fraggle Rock*
6. *Ivor the Engine*
7. *Mary, Mungo and Midge*
8. *Noah and Nelly*
9. *Pogle's Wood*
10. *Supergran*

Don't eat these mushrooms

1. Red staining inocybe
2. Destroying angel
3. Fly agaric
4. Devil's boletus
5. Panther cap
6. Sulphur tuft
7. Death cap
8. The sickener

Man

- Fellow
- Chap
- Geezer
- Bloke
- Guy
- Old boy
- Lad
- Bod
- Character
- Johnny
- Comrade

Ten interesting words beginning with 'Y'

Yabby	A small crayfish
Yackety-yak	Boring talk
Yottameter	10,000,000,000,000,000,000,000,000 metres
Yaffle	A green woodpecker
Yclept	Called
Yegg	A burglar
Yellow-belly	A coward
Ylang-ylang	A scented oil
Yomp	A march over the hills
Yurt	A Mongolian tent

What does your surname mean?

Fletcher	Arrow maker
Spencer	Person in charge of a pantry or storeroom
Reid	Red-haired person
Hardy	A tough warrior
Todd	Like a fox
Dixon	Richard's (Dick's) son
Daniels	From the Bible character (in the lion's den)
Bristow	From the city of Bristol
Winterbottom	A narrow deep valley
Walsh	Welsh, or a foreigner
Dennis	A Danish person

Nine currencies

Currency	Country
Leu	Moldova
Ouguiya	Mauritania
Birr	Ethiopia
Markka	Finland
Vatu	Vanuatu
Tenge	Kazakhstan
Sucre	Ecuador
Gourde	Haiti
Loti	Lesotho

SILLY FACTS

They have never played for Arsenal

Cilla Black	Your auntie
Bob the Builder	A cuttlefish
Henry VIII	Pantaloons

Nine newspapers from around the world

1	*Penguin News*	Falkland Islands
2	*The Survivor*	Botswana
3	*The Mumbai Grapevine*	India
4	*Planet Tonga*	Tonga
5	*Munster Express*	Ireland
6	*Times of Oman*	Oman
7	*The Jamaica Gleaner*	Jamaica
8	*The Buffalo Reflex*	USA
9	*The Holbrook, Billabong and Upper Murray Chronicle*	Australia

Ten snakes to avoid

1 Black Mamba
2 Cobra
3 Rattlesnake
4 Yellow-bellied Sea Snake
5 Tiger Snake
6 Coral Snake
7 Taipan
8 Russell's Viper
9 Boomslang
10 Banded Krait

Former football grounds

Norwich City	The Nest
Falkirk	Blinkbonny
Cambridge United	Parker's Piece
Stranraer	The Trotting Track
Southampton	The Antelope Ground
St Mirren	Shortroods
Lincoln City	The Cow Pat

Five food additives

E120 Cochineal (red colourant) – made from insects
E407 Carrageenan (thickener) – made from seaweed
E416 Karaya Gum (thickener) – made from trees
E413 Tragacanth (emulsifier) – made from plants
E150 Caramel (brown-black colour) – made from sugar

Seven ways to light a fire

1 Matches
2 Cigarette lighter
3 Sunlight through a lens
4 Striking flint
5 Battery (joining the terminals)
6 Rubbing sticks together
7 Gunpowder

Age of some sports

Bowling	7,000 years
Wrestling	4,700 years
Archery	3,500 years
Olympic Games	2,780 years
Tennis	800 years
Football (27-a-side)	600 years
Cricket	260 years
Rugby	180 years
Winter Olympics	80 years
Bungee jumping	15 years

Things you can blow

• Trumpet • Your nose • Hot and cold
• Your mind • Your top • Glass • Bubbles • It

Eight French towns

1 Nancy
2 Albert
3 La Machine
4 Lunéville
5 Brest
6 Sissy
7 Cadillac
8 Berck

Five expressions containing the word

1 A bad egg – *a dodgy person*
2 As sure as eggs is eggs – *said when something is certain*
3 Don't put all your eggs in one basket – *keep your options open*
4 Teach your grandmother to suck eggs – *to try to teach someone something they can already do*
5 An egg head – a *very brainy person*

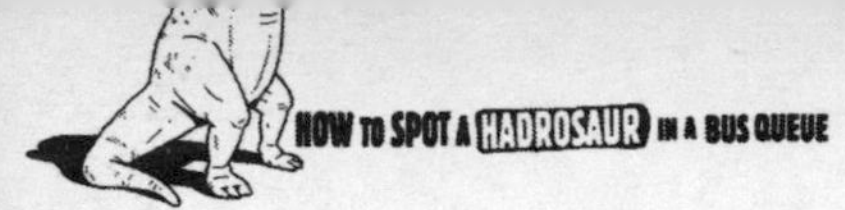

British-American translation

UK	USA
Autumn	Fall
Cotton reel	Spool
Curtains	Drapes
First floor	Second floor
Fringe	Bangs
Kerb	Curb
Nappy	Diaper
Petrol	Gas
Pig	Hog
Tap	Faucet
Trousers	Pants
Pram	Baby carriage
Toilet	Washroom
Maths	Math

11 cartoon exclamations and sounds

1 Yikes!
2 Eek!
3 Ooyah!
4 Grrr!
5 Chomp!
6 Blam!
7 Plop!
8 Swoon!
9 Splat!
10 Thwack!
11 Kerunch!

SILLY FACTS

Six things not to put in your sandwiches

1 Carpet
2 Vaseline
3 Old socks
4 Dynamite
5 Your best friend
6 Bread

22 assorted baddies

1 Captain Hook
2 Blofeld
3 Lex Luther
4 Wile E. Coyote
5 Dracula
6 Judas
7 Darth Vader
8 Doctor Crippen
9 Fagin
10 Blackbeard
11 Mr Hyde
12 Al Capone
13 Herod
14 Sauron
15 Bluto
16 Fu Manchu
17 Dick Dastardly
18 The Joker
19 Dick Turpin
20 The Master
21 Cruella De Ville
22 The Big Bad Wolf

Average TV viewing

USA	30.1 hours per week
Japan	28.3 hours per week
Italy	28 hours per week
Spain	28 hours per week
UK	24.5 hours per week

13 good birds and where you can see them

1	Common Noddy	(South America)
2	Spotted Thick Knee	(Ethiopia)
3	Gang Gang Cockatoo	(Australia)
4	Woolly-necked Stork	(Uganda)
5	Great Potoo	(Brazil)
6	Laughing Jackass	(New Zealand)
7	Whip-poor-will	(Canada)
8	Chin-spot Puffback	(Mozambique)
9	Bare-faced Go-away Bird	(Tanzania)
10	Bully Canary	(Ethiopia)
11	Noisy Leatherhead	(Australia)
12	Owlet Frogmouth	(New Guinea)
13	Racket-tailed Drongo	(Malaysia)

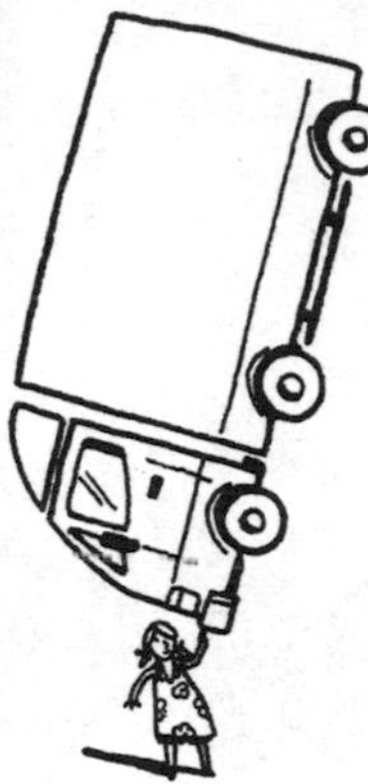

Ten less common girls' names and their meanings

1	Anona	Grace
2	Blodwen	White flower
3	Clotilda	Loud
4	Dodo	Gift of God
5	Dympna	An old Irish name
6	Ermyntrude	Universal strength
7	Lettice	Gladness
8	Myrtle	A flower
9	Oona	An old Irish name
10	Zenobia	A Roman queen

SILLY FACTS

Pap groups

- S Club 2½
- Atomic Tadpole
- Westdeath
- Girls Alas
- Blew
- Mis-take

Eight real places in Wensleydale

1 Barf End Gate
2 Dirty Piece
3 Faggergill Wood
4 Lousy Hill
5 Black Bank Hags
6 Hell Hole Slack
7 Rotten Bottom
8 Dicky Edge

Seven things with holes in

1 Swiss cheese
2 A DVD
3 Underpants
4 A torpedoed beach ball
5 Your head
6 Cornwall
7 A barracuda's bottom

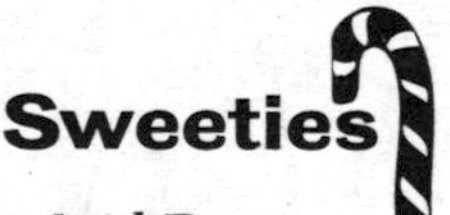

Sweeties

- Acid Drops
- Midget Gems
- Cough Candy
- Banana and Custard
- Dewdrops
- Aniseed Twists
- Bullseyes
- Lemon Bon Bons
- Pineapple Sherbert
- White Mice
- Pontefract Cakes
- Pear Drops

A selection of the world's fastest cars

Year	Car	Engine	Country	Speed
1898	Jeantaud	Electric	France	63 km/h (39 mph)
1902	Serpollet	Steam	France	121 km/h (75 mph)
1903	Gobron-Brillie	Piston	Belgium	137 km/h (85 mph)
1905	Darracq	Piston	France	177 km/h (110 mph)
1910	Lightning Benz	Piston	USA	220 km/h (137 mph)
1926	Sunbeam Tiger	Piston	GB	245 km/h (152 mph)
1927	Sunbeam Slug	Piston	GB	328 km/h (204 mph)
1929	Golden Arrow	Piston	GB	372 km/h (231 mph)
1937	Thunderbolt	Piston	GB	502 km/h (312 mph)
1964	Proteus Blue Bird	Piston	GB	649 km/h (403 mph)
1964	Green Monster	Jet	USA	698 km/h (434 mph)
1965	Spirit of America Sonic 1	Jet	USA	893 km/h (555 mph)
1970	Blue Flame	Rocket	USA	1001 km/h (622 mph)
1983	Thrust 2	Jet	GB	1019 km/h (633 mph)
1997	Thrust SSC	Jet	GB	1228 km/h (763 mph)

Nine horrid mythical creatures

1	Imp	A small naughty creature
2	Bogie	(Also called bogey or bogeyman) a scary monster or spirit
3	Troll	An ugly dwarf or giant, usually living in a cave
4	Sprite	A type of fairy or elf
5	Goblin	A small, mischievous, ugly creature
6	Hag	An old evil woman, often a witch
7	Pixie	A fairy or elf with pointed ears, sometimes naughty
8	Gremlin	A small troublesome creature blamed for faults in machinery
9	Ogre	A wicked man-eating giant

How many wild animals are there in Britain?

Field vole	75 million
Common shrew	42 million
Rabbit	38 million
Mole	31 million
House mouse	5 million
Grey squirrel	2.5 million
Pipistrelle bat	2 million

Notable noses

Pinocchio	Fictional puppet with a wooden nose that grew longer whenever he told lies
The Duke of Wellington	He was called 'Old Nosey' by his troops
Tycho Brahe	This Danish astronomer had a golden nose (he lost his real one in a duel)
Oliver Cromwell	Was known as 'Ruby Nose' because of his large red hooter
Cyrano de Bergerac	A French playwright with an exceptionally long snout
Matthew Parker	One time Archbishop of Canterbury under Elizabeth I, was the original 'Nosey Parker'
Jimmy Durante	An American singer with a bulbous conk who was known as 'Schnozzle'
Joseph Myslivecek	A Czech composer who had no nose (he cut it off attempting to cure an illness)

Eight advertising slogans

It's finger lickin' good	KFC 1953
Full of eastern promise	Fry's Turkish Delight 1950s
Grace... space... pace	Jaguar cars 1950s
Nice one Cyril	Wonderloaf 1972
It's a lot less bovver than a hover	Qualcast Concord mower 1985
Go to work on an egg	British Egg Marketing Board 1957
Put a tiger in your tank	Esso 1964
A little dab'll do ya	Brylcreem 1949

Eight aviation abbreviations

1	AAA	Anti-aircraft artillery
2	AWACS	Airborne warning and control system
3	FBW	Fly by wire
4	HDD	Head down display
5	MTOW	Maximum take-off weight
6	OTH	Over the horizon
7	SAR	Search and rescue
8	VTOL	Vertical take-off and landing

Number of computers connected to the Internet

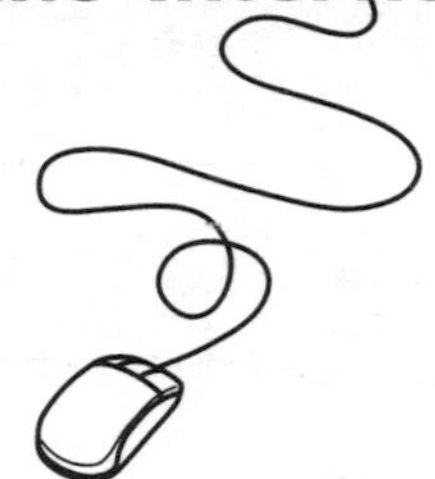

1977	111
1981	213
1983	562
1984	1,000
1986	5,000
1987	10,000
1989	100,000
1992	1 million
2001	170 million
2002	200 million

SILLY FACTS

Misheard proverbs

- The bigger they are, the harder they hit you
- Nothing ventured, nothing lost
- Don't count your chickens until they keep still
- You can't teach an old dog brain surgery
- Don't look a gift horse in the bottom
- Rome wasn't built in a newsagent's
- A leopard cannot change its underpants
- Too many slugs spoil the broth
- There's no place like Hpjkxm

Five interesting numbers

5040

This can be divided by any number from 1 to 10

4! (four bang)

4! = 24 because 4 x 3 x 2 x 1 = 24

---

i

i = $\sqrt{-1}$ (this is called an imaginary number)

---

googol

1 googol = 10^{100} (1 followed by 100 zeros)

18,446,744,073,709,551,651

This number is the answer to the following famous puzzle: how many grains of rice would there be on the last square of a chess board if you put one grain on the first square, 2 grains on the second square, 4 on the third, and so on (doubling the number each time)?

Ten Welsh towns and villages

1 Stepaside
2 Login
3 Clatter
4 Splott
5 Mold
6 Stackpole
7 Pyle
8 Pandy Tudur
9 Nebo
10 Nottage

Eight catchphrases

'Eat my shorts'	Bart Simpson
'And now for something completely different'	*Monty Python*
'Exterminate!'	The Daleks
'What's up doc?'	Bugs Bunny
'I have a cunning plan'	Baldrick
'Yabba dabba doo!'	Fred Flintstone
'Suit you, sir'	*The Fast Show*
'D'oh!'	Homer Simpson

Five sentences not to include in your homework

1 The naughty schoolboy was suspended by the head.

2 I met a man sawing wood with a broken leg.

3 You can drop your trousers at the dry cleaners if they are dirty.

4 I saw a woman with a glass eye called Doris.

5 The police dog chased the man on a bicycle.

Six table tennis bat rubbers

- Tackifire Special
- Curl Bamboo
- Terminator Reverse
- Dr Neubauer Magic Pips
- Double Happiness G888
- Grass Devil Pimples Out

Calories

Food	Calories	Food	Calories
100 g celery	5	100 g scone	335
100 g salad	19	100 g popcorn	405
100 ml orange juice	44	100 g chocolate	530
100 g pizza	210	100 g butter	740
100 g chips	253		

Nine crooners

1. Perry Como
2. Nat King Cole
3. Bing Crosby
4. Pat Boone
5. Frank Sinatra
6. Frankie Laine
7. Andy Williams
8. Dean Martin
9. Mel Torme

11 films you've probably never seen

1. *The Cars That Ate Paris* (1974)
2. *Attack of the 50-Foot Woman* (1958)
3. *The Teenage Frankenstein Meets the Teenage Werewolf* (1959)
4. *Around the Equator on Roller Skates* (1932)
5. *Dooley's Thanksgiving Turkey* (1909)
6. *The Foot Shooting Party* (1994)
7. *When Father Had the Gout* (1915)
8. *The Midnight Bum* (1927)
9. *The Ghost in the Invisible Bikini* (1966)
10. *When Eddie Took a Bath* (1915)
11. *I'll Never Forget What's 'is Name* (1967)

Three

3-point turn
3 musketeers
3-piece suite
3 wise men
3-D
3 cheers
3-card trick
3 Rs
3-wheeler
3 blind mice
3-legged race

How to say 'yes' in 13 languages

Albanian	Po
Armenian	Ha
Danish	Ja
Finnish	Kyllä
French	Oui
Greek	Ne
Mandarin Chinese	Shi
Mongolian	Tiim
Punjabi	Han ji
Russian	Da
Spanish	Si
Thai	Chai
Zulu	Yebo

Meaning of place names

Wallsend	Settlement at the end of Hadrian's Wall
Ely	Place of eels
Blackpool	Used to have a black pool
Troon	Means nose
Nottingham	Settlement of Snott's people

SILLY FACTS

Things not invented by Leonardo

- Cup a Soup
- Knees
- Deelyboppers
- Those funny orange lawnmowers
- Belgium

Individuals' trademarks

Cane	Charlie Chaplin
Dummy	Maggie Simpson
Pointy hat	Gandalf
Whip	Indiana Jones
Striped jumper	Dennis the Menace
Corgis	The Queen
Elephant	Hannibal
Quiff	Elvis
Lamp	Florence Nightingale
White beard	Santa
Cigar	Groucho Marx
Bowler hats	Laurel and Hardy
Scarf	Dr Who
Hook	Captain Hook
Deerstalker	Sherlock Holmes

Secret organisations

The Know Nothings	A secret American political party of the 19th century, which tried to prevent foreigners from becoming important. People accused of being members of the organisation used to say, 'I know nothing.'
MI6	The British Secret Intelligence Service, involved with spying and undercover operations abroad. MI5 is known as the Security Service, and carries out secret work in the UK; MI stands for Military Intelligence.
Freemasons	An international organisation made up of groups of men, called Lodges (the groups not the men), who help one another. Freemasons sometimes hold special secret ceremonies involving daggers.
KGB	The secret police of the former Soviet Union, who spied on anyone suspected of not being loyal to the government. KGB is short for *Komitet Gosudarstvennoi Bezopasnosti*.

The Mafia	An assortment of criminal groups which began in Sicily. The Mafia spread to Italy and America, and became involved with illegal guns, gambling and drugs among other things.
The Secret Service	American law enforcement organisation. Its agents protect the President, and prevent the forgery of US money.
Ku Klux Klan	Illegal secret organisation formed in the USA in the 1800s, committed to terrorizing black people. They wore white robes and pointed hats, and used the symbol of a burning cross.
Gestapo	Hitler's secret police run by Hermann Göring. They arrested, tortured, imprisoned and killed opponents of the Nazis.

Nine polite words for 'bum'

1 Bottom
2 Rear
3 Backside
4 Posterior
5 Behind
6 Derriere
7 Seat
8 Buttocks
9 Situpon

SILLY FACTS

Strange, but false

- The Venezuelan sloth has a spare foot, which it keeps in a bush
- Belgians make an interesting after-dinner snack
- You can test if your Great Aunt is electric by removing her battery
- Any pastry product wider than 72.4 cm requires a licence from the police
- The record length for a school assembly is 15 days
- In 1928, a netball match was abandoned when the umpire was abducted by feral handymen
- North of Spitzbergen, it is illegal to operate a ladle between the hours of 6pm and 9am

Brief animal lives

Giant centipede	10 years
Purse web spider	9 years
House mouse	6 years
Moon rat	4½ years
Pygmy shrew	2½ years
Bedbug	6 months
Housefly	15 days
Adult mayfly	1 day

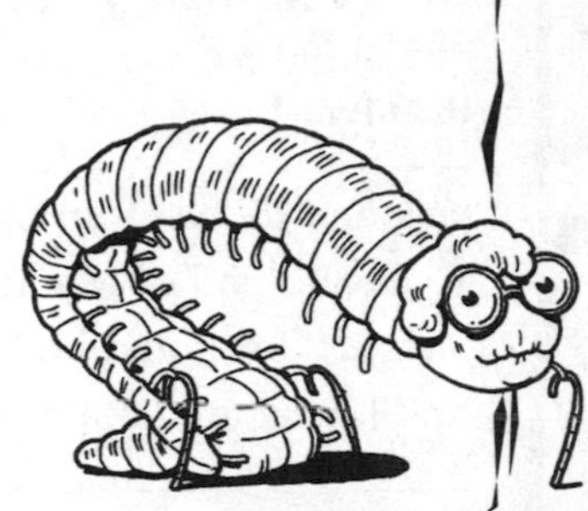

Well-known wheels

James Bond	Aston Martin DB-5
Lady Penelope	Pink 6-wheel Rolls-Royce
Batman	Batmobile
Caractacus Potts	Chitty Chitty Bang Bang
Mr Bean	Yellowy green mini
Del Boy and Rodney Trotter	Reliant 3-wheeler van
Harry Potter	Ford Anglia
Jim Douglas	Herbie (VW Beetle)
Inspector Morse	Mk II Jaguar
Scooby Doo	The Mystery Machine
Michael Schumacher	F1 Ferrari
Noddy	Noddy Car

SILLY FACTS

Nursery rhyme solutions

Problem	Solution
Jack and Jill went up the hill To fetch a pail of water; Jack fell down and broke his crown And Jill came tumbling after.	Get water from Tesco
Little Bo Peep has lost her sheep And doesn't know where to find them.	Keep sheep in a large box
Old Mother Hubbard Went to the cupboard To fetch her poor dog a bone; But when she got there; The cupboard was bare; And so the poor doggie had none.	Swap dog for DVD player
Little Miss Muffet sat on a tuffet Eating her curds and whey; Along came a spider Who sat down beside her And frightened Miss Muffet away.	Avoid tuffets

Problem	Solution
Dr Foster went to Gloucester In a shower of rain; He stepped in a puddle Right up to his middle And never went there again.	Use a 4x4
Rock a bye baby on the tree top; When the wind blows, the cradle will rock; When the bow breaks the cradle will fall, Down will come cradle, baby and all.	Superglue cradle to branch
London Bridge is falling down, Falling down, falling down; London Bridge is falling down, My fair lady.	Go to Sidcup

Hard winters

1684	Horse-drawn coaches travelled along the frozen River Thames
1739-40	Snow fell for 39 days in SE England
1947	Snowdrifts were 5 metres deep in the hills of northern Britain
1952	Smog (smoke mixed with fog) killed 4,000 people in London
1962-63	Most of England was covered by snow from December to March
1963	Parts of the sea froze off the south coast
1978	A train in Scotland was completely buried by snow

16 old car makers

1. Wartburg
2. Alldays and Onions
3. Spycker
4. Bow-v-car
5. Bean
6. Crypto
7. BAT
8. Dolly
9. Frisky
10. Gnome
11. Magnetic
12. Nameless
13. De P
14. Willys
15. Gogomobil
16. Le Zebre

Good tunes

Da-da-da daaaa	Beethoven's 5th Symphony
Tum-ti tum-ti tum-ti tum	*The Archers* theme
De-dum de-dum de-dum de-dum-de-dum-de-dum	*The Pink Panther* theme
Nahhh nah nah nah-na-na-nah	*The Dambusters* theme
La la la laa-la-laa, la la la Laa-la-laa, laa laa laa-laa	The National Anthem
Daaaa da-daa da-da-daaa	*Coronation Street* theme
Deed-li deed-li deed-li dee-dee	William Tell Overture

SILLY FACTS

Causes of sock loss

1 Hole in heel
2 Elastic failure
3 Toe emergence
4 Washing machine incident
5 Unreasonable shrinkage
6 Fashion withdrawal

SILLY FACTS

Helpful advice

- If you arrive at school late, make up for it by leaving early
- Never put your false teeth in backwards or you might eat yourself
- Remember you can't buy a car boot at a car boot sale
- If at first you don't succeed, avoid skydiving
- A chicken which is still clucking is probably undercooked
- If you are on a diet, a simple way to lose 5 kg is to cut off a leg
- When you are attacked by a bear, lie down and pretend to be dead; when attacked by margarine, lie down and pretend to be bread

Puppets

- Captain Scarlet
- Sooty & Sweep
- Mr Punch
- Kermit
- Basil Brush
- Pinocchio
- Cookie Monster
- Looby-Lou
- Bill & Ben
- Scott Tracy
- Fingermouse
- Zippy
- Emu
- Andy Pandy

The Mount St Helens volcano eruption

When	1980
Where	Washington State, USA
What happened	A mega volcanic eruption
Main blast	Blew 396 metres off the top of the mountain
Area of total destruction	13 km (8 miles) in all directions
Trees knocked over	Millions, up to 27 km (17 miles) away
What came out of the volcano	Ash cloud, mud flow, ice, rock landslide
Height of ash cloud	18,000 m
Amount of ash	540 million tonnes
Speed of rock landslide	113-241 km/h (70-150 mph)
Depth of rock burying Toutle River	60 m
How far away explosion was heard	322 km (200 miles)

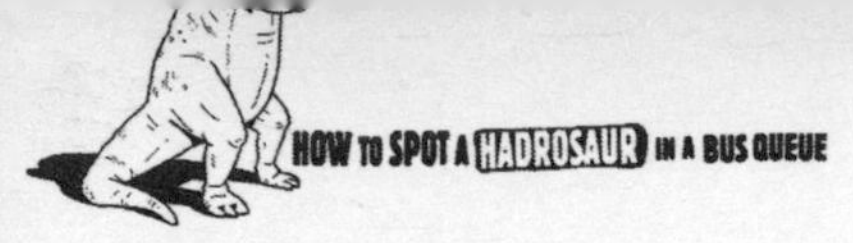

Calendar nuggets

- For many centuries in Britain and America, New Year's Day was on 25th March
- The actual length of a year is 365 days, 5 hours, 48 minutes, 45 seconds
- Years are becoming shorter over time at the rate of 1/2 second per century due to the slowing of the Earth's rotation
- In the 1600s, Britain used a different calendar to most of Europe, causing a great deal of confusion about dates
- The world did not agree on what the date was until 1949 when China began to use the western calendar
- From 1792-1806, the French introduced a new calendar. It had 12 equal months of 30 days; 5 or 6 holidays; 3 weeks per month each 10 days long; 10 hours in a day, each 100 minutes long, and 100 seconds in a minute
- The eastern Orthodox Church still uses Julius Caesar's Roman calendar, developed 2000 years ago
- In the year 4909, our present calendar will be a day ahead of the true (solar) year

Pop stars called Norman

Norman Wisdom	1954
Norman Brooks	1954
Norman Vaughan	1962
Norman Greenbaum	1970
Norman Cook	1989
Norman Bass	2001

Toy milestones

1759	Roller Skates
1840	Mass-produced dolls
1896	Ludo
1902	Teddy bears
1903	Crayons
1913	Construction kits
1929	Yo-yo
1931	Scrabble
1936	Monopoly
1949	Lego
1952	Matchbox cars
1959	Barbie
1960	Etch-a-Sketch
1971	Space Hopper
1973	Mastermind
1977	Slime
1979	Rubik's Cube
1986	Pictionary
1993	Beanie Babies
2003	Bart Simpson Radio Control Skateboard

Asterix's contemporaries

Obelix	Big, unfeasibly strong Gaul
Dogmatix	Asterix's mini-mongrel pooch
Getafix	Druid and magic potion man
Cacofonix	The village's bad, bad bard
Vitalstatistix	Ball-shaped village chief
Geriatrix	Village fogey
Fulliautomatix	Bad-tempered blacksmith
Unhygienix	Pongsome village fishmonger
Impedimentia	Elegant wife of the village chief
Bacteria	The fishmonger's delightful wife
Julius Caesar	Heavy-nosed Roman general
Crismus Bonus	Mean centurion

What they call the English

Aussies	Poms
Scots	Sassenachs
Americans	Limeys (in World War II)
French	Rosbifs
Various	Brits
French	Les Anglais

Bizarre festivals

World Ice Golf Championship	Greenland
Interstate Mullet Toss	Florida, USA
Camel Wrestling Festival	Selcuk, Turkey
Snowman Burning	Michigan, USA
World Bog Snorkelling Championship	Llanwrtyd Wells, Wales
The Annual Doo Dah Parade	Ohio, USA
La Tomatina (tomato fight with 10,000 people)	Bunol, Spain
Cooper's Hill Cheese Roll	Gloucestershire, England
Air Guitar World Championships	Finland
Nude Olympics	Arizona, USA
World Lying Championships	Cumbria, England

Eight explosives

1 Gunpowder
2 Nitroglycerine
3 TNT
4 Dynamite
5 Saltpetre
6 Gelignite
7 Guncotton
8 Rippite

SILLY FACTS

They don't need one

David Beckham	Number in the phone book
Aston Villa	Trophy cabinet
Giraffe	Periscope
Pierluigi Collina	Barber
Switzerland	Coastguard
Tree	Passport
Mike Tyson	Bodyguard
Haddock	Bra

Hefty beasts

Animal	Weighs the same as this many people
Yak	11
Kodiak bear	11
Saltwater crocodile	16
Giraffe	17
Hippo	29
White rhino	31
African elephant	71
Blue whale	2,714

Accidents in 1999

Cause	Number of UK accidents
Meat cleavers	329
Tree trunks	1,810
Rat poison	439
Sofas	16,662
Wellies	5,615
Bird baths	311
Chainsaws	1,207
Trousers	5,945
Vegetables	13,132
Socks and tights	10,773
Talcum powder	73
Toilet roll holders	329
Place mats	165
Bread bins	91

Eight countries beginning and ending with 'A'

1 Albania
2 Algeria
3 Andorra
4 Angola
5 Argentina
6 Armenia
7 Australia
8 Austria

17 places in New Zealand

1 All Day Bay
2 Alligator Bay
3 Cannibal Bay
4 Kakepuku
5 Kiriwhakapapa
6 Knuckles
7 Kuku
8 No Man's Land
9 Orangiponga
10 Poison Bay
11 Pukapuka
12 Puketoetoe
13 Taumatawhakatangiha-ngakoauotamateapokai-whenuakitanatahu
14 Puni
15 Te Puke
16 Whakapapataringa
17 Whangamumu

Where to find lots of roads

USA	6,328,000 km (3,932,219 miles)
Russia	1,588,000 km (986,783 miles)
Japan	1,120,000 km (695,968 miles)
France	811,000 km (503,955 miles)
Germany	549,000 km (341,149 miles)
UK	380,000 km (236,132 miles)

15 Elizabeth diminutives

1 Bess
2 Bessie
3 Ella
4 Elsie
5 Beth
6 Betsy
7 Betty
8 Eliza
9 Libby
10 Lilian
11 Lisa
12 Lisbeth
13 Liz
14 Liza
15 Lizzie

SILLY FACTS

What do you call a woman with...

a cat on her head?	Kitty
a tortoise on her head?	Shelley
fishing gear on her head?	Annette
a pond on her head?	Lily
two toilets on her head?	Lulu
a coffin on her head?	Di
a beach on her head?	Sandy
a monastery on her head?	Abi
a breeze on her head?	Gail
a radiator on her head?	Anita
a judge on her head?	Sue
the sun on her head?	Dawn

British accents

BBC Standard English	Right
Brummie	Roight
Scots	Reet
Cockney	Roih'
West Country	Roy'
Yorkshire	Rart
Welsh	Reight
Scouse	Riter
Irish	Roite
Geordie	Rait

Pet fame

- The Roman emperor Nero kept a tiger called Phoebe
- The composer Mozart owned a starling
- Queen Victoria had a pug called Bully
- Writer Lord Byron kept a bear in his rooms at college
- Doctor Albert Schweitzer possessed an antelope called Theodore
- Winston Churchill had a cat called Margate
- US President John F. Kennedy owned a hamster called Billie
- Pop star Michael Jackson kept a monkey called Bubbles

Trade names

Audi	Means 'hear' in Latin – the car was developed by Dr Horch whose name also means 'hear'
Birds Eye	Named after Clarence Birdseye, an inventor of food freezing methods
Coca-Cola	The drink contains parts of coca nuts and cola leaves
Uhu	The German word for eagle owl – found near the factory in the Black Forest
Esso	From S.O., an abbreviation for Standard Oil
Fanta	Short for fantasy
Granada	The company chairman went on holiday to Spain in the 1920s and was very impressed by the city of Granada
Kenwood	The founder of the company was called Ken Wood
Lego	From the Danish words *leg godt*, meaning 'play well'
Oxo	From the animal, ox
Sanyo	Japanese for three oceans
Trebor	The company founder, Robert Robertson, spelt his first name backwards

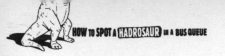

11 real comics

1 *Merv Pumpkinhead: Agent of D.E.A.T.H.*
2 *Accident Man*
3 *Biker Mice from Mars*
4 *Captain Carrot*
5 *Ectokid*
6 *Giant Size Man-Thing*
7 *Lethargic Lad*
8 *Propellerman*
9 *Sludge*
10 *Too Much Coffee Man*
11 *Yawn*

Prepay deals

Mobiles	Pay as you go
Trumpets	Pay as you blow
Lawns	Pay as you mow
Candles	Pay as you glow
Rivers	Pay as you flow
Spears	Pay as you throw
Boats	Pay as you row
Professors	Pay as you know
Blizzards	Pay as you snow
Old bangers	Pay as you tow

11 Monty Python creations

1 The Ministry of Silly Walks
2 Spam Spam Spam
3 Albatross!
4 Dead Parrot Sketch
5 Upper Class Twit of the Year
6 Nudge nudge, wink wink
7 The Cheese Shop
8 Gumbys
9 Give me your lupins
10 I'm a lumberjack
11 Four Yorkshiremen Sketch

Some of the things in a top Harrods' hamper

- Champagne
- Venison pâté
- Quail eggs
- Brandy butter
- Teapot
- Brown Swizzle Sticks
- Tea towel
- Chocolate Lemon Discs
- Coffee mugs

Races in 2004

Race	Type	When	Where
One Lap of America	Cars	May	Right round USA
British Lawn Mower Grand Prix	Lawn mowers	Oct	Sussex, UK
Australia Day Cockroach Races	Cockroaches	Jan	Brisbane, Australia
The Cresta Run	Toboggans	Dec-Feb	St Moritz, Switzerland
Chon Buri Buffalo Races	Buffaloes	Oct	Chon Buri, Thailand
Florida Swamp Buggy International Classic	Swamp buggies	Jan	Florida, USA
London to Sydney Car Rally	Cars	Jun	Across the world
Clearlake International Worm Races	Worms	Jul	California, USA
Sharm El-Sheik Camel Race	Camels	May	Sharm El-Sheik, Egypt
Empire State Building Marathon	Race up the stairs	Feb	New York, USA

Ten fine Irish place names

1 Ballydehob
2 Benburb
3 Stoneybatter
4 Kilkenny
5 Clones
6 Knock
7 Coolgreaney
8 Glasheencoombaun
9 Ovens
10 Slemish

SILLY FACTS

FAQs

Where do you find Golden Eagles?	It depends where you left them
How many months have 28 days?	All of them
Why do birds fly south in winter?	It's too far to walk
Where are the Andes?	At the end of your armies
What's the capital of Portugal?	P
What question can you never answer 'yes' to?	Are you asleep?
Can a kangaroo jump higher than a house?	Yes – houses can't jump
Who knocked down the walls of Jericho?	It wasn't me, honest
How do you keep flies out of the kitchen?	Put a bucket of poo in the living room

Expensive buys at auction

Item	What exactly	How much?	When
Cup	Ming porcelain chicken cup	£1.9 million	1999
Book	*The Gospel of Henry the Lion*	£8.1 million	1983
Costume	Original *Superman* film costume	£13,000	1999
Car	Ferrari 250 GTO	£6.4 million	1990
Coin	1933 Double Eagle $20 gold coin	£3.9 million	2002
Bottle of wine	1998 Penfold's Grange Australian wine	£29,000	2003
Vase	Qing Dynasty Chinese peach-patterned vase	£2.7 million	2002
Ball	Football used in the 1888 FA Cup Final	£32,900	2002
Drawing	Leonardo's sketch of a horse and rider	£8.1 million	2001
Teddy	1904 Teddy Girl bear	£110,000	1994
Violin	1736 Stradivarius violin	£767,000	2003
Document	Print of US Declaration of Independence	£4.2 million	2000
Painting	Van Gogh's portrait of Dr Gachet	£54.2 million	1990

Henrys

- Enrico — Italy
- Henri — France
- Henrique — Portugal
- Hendrik — Holland
- Heikki — Finland
- Enrique — Spain
- Henricus — Latin
- Henrik — Sweden
- Henning — Denmark
- Heinrich — Germany
- Hainrich — Poland

15 dances

1 Cha-cha-cha
2 Flamenco
3 Jive
4 Cakewalk
5 Calypso
6 Jitterbug
7 Turkey Trot
8 Cancan
9 Jig
10 Gagaku
11 Tango
12 Limbo
13 Rumba
14 Samba
15 Conga

Computer game timeline

1952	World's first computer game – a version of noughts and crosses
1961	*Spacewar* – first computer game to be sold
1973	*Pong* – simple arcade game
1975	*Adventure* – first text-based adventure game
1978	*Space Invaders* – successful arcade game
1980	*Mario* – first appears in *Donkey Kong*
1988	Game Boy – handheld game
1989	Sega Megadrive – early console
1990	*Sonic the Hedgehog*
1993	Sony PlayStation
1995	Nintendo 64
1995	*Tomb Raider*
1997	Sega Dreamcast
2000	PlayStation 2
2001	Microsoft Xbox
2002	Nintendo Gamecube

Old school punishment weapons

Birch	A bunch of thin branches applied to bare buttocks only
Cane	Classic flexible stick used on hand or bottom
Ruler	Cracked across the palm (wooden model preferred)
Slipper	Usually a plimsoll or gym shoe: flexible and painful
Hand	For 'clip around the ear' or similar
Board rubber	Usually thrown for rapid response punishment
Register	For sharp whack on the head; heavier books also used
Strap	Strip of leather used for whipping
Tawse	Split leather strap used on the hand once 'popular' in Scotland
Belt	Similar to strap and tawse. Nasty.

The most popular colours for front doors

1 Blue	3 White	5 Green
2 Red	4 Black	6 Yellow

Museums worth a visit

Potty Museum	Munich, Germany
Museum of Questionable Medical Devices	Minnesota, USA
Comic Museum	Brussels, Belgium
The Toaster Museum Foundation	Charlottesville, USA
Spy Museum	Tampere, Finland
Toilet Seat Museum	Texas, USA
Sock Museum	Sakata, Japan
Banana Museum	Auburn, USA
Cheese Museum	Hawes, UK
Museum of Hoaxes	online
Museum of Coathangers	online
Museum of Unusual X-rays	online
The Sugar Packet Collection	online
Graham Barker's Navel Fluff Collection	online

SILLY FACTS

Drivers to avoid

Driver	Vehicle
Man in hat	Brown 1975 Austin Allegro
Gangster	Lamborghini towing a caravan
Cigar smoker	Open wagon full of dynamite
Learner	Stretch limo
Monster	Monster truck
Boy racer	Sofa delivery moped
Dog	Any

Yorkshirespeak

Now then	Hello
Ayup	Look!
Sithee	Bye
Put plug int t'ole	Shut the door
Jiggered	Worn out
Fair t'middlin	Alright
Nous	Sense
Sup	To drink
A reet ding-dong	A big argument
Dollop	Lump

14 cheeses of the world

Sardo	Argentina
Kangaroo Island	Australia
Tilsit	Germany
Sap Sago	Switzerland
Gorgonzola	Italy
Kasseri	Greece
Fontina	Denmark
Lappi	Finland
Knockalara	Ireland
Longhorn	USA
Mimolette	France
Swinzie	Scotland
Graddost	Sweden
Tetilla	Spain

Five things that will not stop a tsunami

1. Wool
2. Singing ‘It’s a Long Way to Tipperary’
3. A selection of after-dinner mints
4. Looking cross
5. Your best friend’s cat

Nine Homer quotes

1 'I hope I didn't brain my damage.'
2 'They have the Internet on computers now?'
3 'I don't apologise – I'm sorry Lisa, that's the way I am.'
4 'Operator! Give me the number for 911.'
5 'Don't eat me – I have a wife and kids. Eat them.'
6 'You'll have to speak up; I'm wearing a towel.'
7 'If something's hard to do then it's not worth doing.'
8 'The sun? That's the hottest place on earth!'
9 'We're going to Moe's. If we're not back, avenge our deaths.'

Doubtful ailments

- Twisted blood
- The heeby-jeebies
- Cabin fever
- The jitters
- A bone in the leg
- The evil eye
- Dartitis
- The willies

12 free things

1	Freebie	Something given away for nothing
2	Freebooter	A pirate
3	Free climbing	Rock climbing without lots of equipment
4	Free fall	Falling with the force of gravity
5	Free-for-all	A situation where everyone can take part
6	Freelancer	A person who works for many different companies
7	Freepost	A letter which doesn't need a stamp
8	Free-range	A farm animal that is allowed to roam around
9	Free-standing	A structure that has no support
10	Freestyle	A sport where competitors choose their own moves
11	Freeware	Free computer software
12	Freeway	US motorway or dual carriageway

Kings who aren't really kings

King of Spades	Playing card
King of the forest	Oak tree
King of the Hill	TV show
King Lear	Play
King Cobra	Snake
King of the mountains	Tour de France bike rider
King Kong	Whopping-great ape
King of cheeses	Roquefort or Stilton
King Charles Spaniel	Dog
King of the beasts	Lion
King Vidor	Film director
King Penguin	Penguin
King of Rock & Roll	Elvis

Eight thrash metal bands

1. Metallica
2. Slayer
3. Machinehead
4. Vomitous Upheaval
5. Agent Steel
6. Xphyxia
7. Anthrax
8. Oomph!

A small assortment of battles

Battle of Marathon	490 BC	Greeks *v.* Persians
Battle of the Standard	1138	Scots *v.* English
Battle of the Herrings	1429	French *v.* English
Battle of the Giants	1515	Francis I *v.* various others
Battle of Fort Necessity	1754	French & Indians *v.* Virginians
Battle of Cowpens	1781	English *v.* Americans
Battle of the Nations	1813	Russians, Prussians, Austrians & Swedish *v.* French
Battle of Britain	1940	British *v.* Germans

Really scary rollercoasters

Name	Location	Watch out for...
Steel Dragon	Nagashima, Japan	the drop of nearly 100 metres
Top Thrill Dragster	Ohio, USA	the tallest point is 128 metres high
The Ultimate	Lightwater Valley, UK	2.7 km of track
Dodonpa	Fujikyu, Japan	travels at over 161 km/h (100 mph)
Nemesis	Alton Towers, UK	a corkscrew ride which goes underground
Oblivion	Alton Towers, UK	a vertical drop
The Missile	American Adventure, UK	turns you upside down six times

Food words

- Grub
- Scoff
- Tucker
- Nosh
- Eats
- Fare
- Tack
- Chow
- Tuck
- Din-dins

Sporting superstitions

Name	Sport	Peculiar habit
Jelena Dokic	Tennis	Wears the same gear through a whole tournament... phew...
Adrian Mutu	Football	Wears his underpants inside out
Jake Matlala	Boxing	Smears his body with chicken blood three weeks before a fight
Marion Jones	Athletics	Jumps on her bed for five minutes the night before events
Mickey Edwards	Rugby League	Places a small model of Thomas the Tank Engine down his socks before a match
Goran Ivanisevic	Tennis	Always eats fish, soup, lamb and ice cream in the same restaurant before Wimbledon matches
Sergio Goycochea	Football	Pees on the pitch before a penalty is taken
Turk Wendell	Baseball	Will only pitch the ball with a mouth full of liquorice
Bruce Gardiner	Ice Hockey	Dips his hockey stick into the toilet before each game

13 pies

- Cow Pie (Desperate Dan's favourite)
- Tree Pie (a bird)
- Porky pie (a lie)
- Moose Pie (scoffed in Canada)
- Humble pie (what you 'eat' as an apology)
- *Alligator Pie* (a poetry book)
- Black Bottom Pie (munched in the States)
- Tweety Pie (Yellow cartoon bird, persecuted by Sylvester the cat)
- Giblet Pie (a Cornish Christmas 'treat')
- German Shepherd Dog Pie (no, it's *for* the dog...)
- *American Pie* (a rude film)
- Eskimo Pie (an ice cream)
- Custard pie (frequently thrown in old silent films)

Giants

Giant anteater	Has a tongue up to 60 cm long
Giant tortoise	Weighs up to 200 kg
Giant clam	Can measure 1 m across
Giant moa	Extinct bird up to 4 m tall
Giant panda	Measures up to 1.9 m long
Giant armadillo	Weighs up to 50 kg
Giant bullfrog	Grows up to 20 cm long
Giant snail	Has a shell up to 20 cm in length
Giant squid	Can reach a length of 18 m

Cat-based sayings

Look what the cat's dragged in	Said to a person having a bad hair day or similar
No room to swing a cat	Describes a very small space such as a titchy room
It's raining cats and dogs	Be careful not to step in a poodle...
Like a cat on a hot tin roof	Very edgy, uneasy, restless (you get the picture)
The cat's whiskers	Top notch; fab; the highest quality
Grin like a Cheshire cat	*Alice in Wonderland* featured a grinning Cheshire cat
Let the cat out of the bag	To reveal a secret. Whoops...
Put the cat among the pigeons	To stir up a load of bother
When the cat's away, the mice will play	Naughty no-nos happen when the boss is absent
The cat's got your tongue	You're speechless

SILLY FACTS

Haddock favourites

Book	Goodbye Mr Chips
Film	A View to a Krill
TV programme	The Weakest Shrimp
Pop group	Codzone
Meal	Toast
Footballer	Paul Shoals
Holiday	The Caribbean
Saying	A rolling stone gathers no haddock

One name's enough

Kylie	Lulu	Posh	Pythagoras
Elton	Sting	Tutankhamun	Jordan
Maggie	Cher	Elvis	Cliff
Dido	Madonna	Britney	Prince
Wills	Moses	Oprah	Adam
Rembrandt	Napoleon	Becks	Michelangelo
Sven	Pele	Houdini	
Gazza	Bono	Bjork	

Britart

Artist	Example of work	Description
Marc Quinn	*Self*	Sculpture of the artist's head made from 5.1 litres (nine pints) of his own frozen blood
Tracy Emin	*My Bed*	The artist's actual bed complete with dirty sheets and old knickers
Damien Hirst	*Some Comfort...*	Cows cut up with chainsaws and preserved in glass tanks of formaldehyde
Sam Taylor-Wood	*Atlantic*	Video of two people having an argument
Cerith Wyn Evans	*TIX3*	A neon exit sign hung back to front
Rachel Whiteread	*Untitled (Torso)*	A plaster cast of the inside of a hot water bottle

SILLY FACTS

Mythical mythological beasts

Scarius	Creature with an ant's body and an elephant's head: quite slow
Brianotaur	Half-man, half-lamp post
Nudra	Half-lion, half-dressed
Springon	Giant flea: no head but 4 bottoms
Cyclots	Race of huge men-like beasts with a single nose in the middle of their faces
Verk	A flying whale with a rhino's horn, tiger's skin and two surface-to-air missiles
Ribbix	Half-cow, half-frog, but divided lengthways: always in a bad mood

10 Downing Street...

- has an underground tunnel connected to Buckingham Palace
- was once owned by a Mr Chicken
- has 160 rooms
- is over 400 years old
- had one of the first TV sets in the world
- was once lived in by the Duke of Wellington
- was bombed in World War II, and in 1991 by the IRA
- once had its telephones bugged by a London gang leader

Clothes that hardly anyone wears any more

- Wimples
- Spats
- Bum rolls
- Jerkins
- Breeches
- Muffs
- Bodices
- Plus fours
- Sack dresses
- Pop socks
- Tank tops
- Shell suits

Overrated things

- Holidays in a wardrobe
- Paper wellies
- Swiss Army forks
- Glass hammers
- Barbed wire underpants
- A third elbow
- Cotton wool bricks
- The book 'Around the World in 80 Hip Replacements'

Jacqueline Wilson central characters

Girl	Book
Jayni	*Lola Rose*
Daisy	*Sleepovers*
Tracy	*The Story of Tracy Beaker*
Ruby & Garnet	*Double Act*
Andy	*The Suitcase Kid*
Dolphin	*The Illustrated Mum*
Mandy	*Bad Girls*
Sadie	*The Mum Minder*

Ten things Roald Dahl did

1. Grew orchids
2. Worked with Walt Disney
3. Dreamt in Norwegian
4. Played billiards
5. Wrote the screenplay for a *James Bond* film
6. Bred budgies
7. Owned two metal hips
8. Invented a medical valve to help people with brain damage
9. Flew Hurricanes in World War II
10. Always wrote on yellow paper

11 doctors

Dr Dolittle	Spoke with the animals
Dr Watson	Sherlock Holmes' trusty assistant
Dr Livingstone	African missionary, I presume
Dr Foster	Went to Gloucester (once)
Dr Julius Hibbert	The Simpsons' family physician
Dr Who	Hero of the BBC's sci-fi series
Dr Pepper	US fizzy drink
Dr No	Villain of first *James Bond* movie
Dr Feelgood	Cheesy 1970s band
Dr Jekyll	Nasty Mr Hyde's alter ego
Dr Seuss	Writer of *The Cat in the Hat*

Uses of human urine

- Making compost
- Cleaning wool
- Lubricant
- Cleaning teeth
- Steel and iron hardener
- Tanning leather
- Cure for earwax
- Washing faces

Classic moustaches

Name	Features	Sported by
Handlebar	Wide and thick with ends curving up	Terry Thomas (British actor)
Pencil	Very thin and pointy	Errol Flynn (American actor)
Walrus	A big, long, bushy, drooping job	Merv Hughes (Aussie cricketer)
Hitler	Small and square	Charlie Chaplin (film star)
Toothbrush	Short, bristly and rectangular	Mr Potato Head (toy figure)
Horseshoe	Very long drooping style	Yosemite Sam (cartoon cowboy)
Dali	Long and thin with waxed razor-sharp ends pointing upwards	Salvador Dali (Spanish painter)
Mexican Bandit	Thick and wide, pointing down at the ends	Mexican bandits
Groucho	Thick, bushy and rectangular	Ned Flanders (The Simpsons' neighbour)

How much coastline?

Canada	243,790 km (151,491 miles)
Australia	25,760 km (16,007 miles)
UK	12,430 km (7,724 miles)
France	3,430 km (2,131 miles)
Romania	225 km (140 miles)
Belgium	64 km (40 miles)
Monaco	4 km (2½ miles)
Austria	0 km (0 miles)

Nine creatures from *The Lord of the Rings*

The Nazgul	Nine black riders
Orcs	Ugly goblin soldiers
Balrog	Harsh Fire spirit
Trolls	Big monsters
Ents	Ancient tree-like chaps
Shelob	Giant spider
Shadowfax	Gandalf's horse
Gwaihar	Lord of the eagles
Gollum	Evil hobbit

Eight Chinese proverbs

- Three feet of ice does not result from one day of bad weather
- Good words are like a string of pearls
- Forget injuries, never forget kindnesses
- A journey of a thousand miles begins with a single step
- When you fall, it isn't your foot's fault
- Talk does not cook the rice
- He who asks is a fool for five minutes, but he who does not ask remains a fool forever
- Do not remove a fly from your friend's head with a hatchet

Nobel prizes

USA	270	Finland	2
UK	100	Burma	1
Germany	77	Indonesia	0
Netherlands	15		

Annoying bodily things

Hiccups	When a twitching diaphragm (your main breathing muscle), causes your glottis (the flappy bit at the top of your throat) to suddenly close
Sneezing	The result of something irritating your nose or nasal passages, such as pollen, causing an explosive expulsion of air
Burps	Caused by air getting into the oesophagus when you swallow, and simply coming back up
Stitch	Probably due to a low blood supply to the diaphragm during exercise – but no one knows for sure
Cramp	When the muscles stiffen or contract on their own (a spasm)
Funny bone	If you hit the ulnar nerve at the back of your elbow it produces a pain down your arm (so don't hit it)

Trumping	The phenomenon caused by air you've swallowed, or gas produced in your gut, being expelled out the back way, through your bottom
Pins & needles	When pressure on a nerve changes electrical signals to the brain, giving a tingly sensation
Cough	A reflex (automatic) response from the body when air is suddenly expelled from the lungs because something is irritating the throat or windpipe, such as dust
Rumbling tum	Caused by gases and digestive juices sloshing around in an empty stomach when its walls squeeze together
Deadleg	The result of a leg muscle being squashed in an injury, causing it to tighten
Goosepimples	If you're chilly, muscles under your skin cause hairs to stand on end so they can trap warm air

So now you know

Index